EDINBURGH
THE FABULOUS
FIFTIES

I Princes Street with the roof of the old
Waverley Market in the foreground.
Postcard view circa 1950

II Princes Street and the National Galleries
from a contemporary coloured postcard.

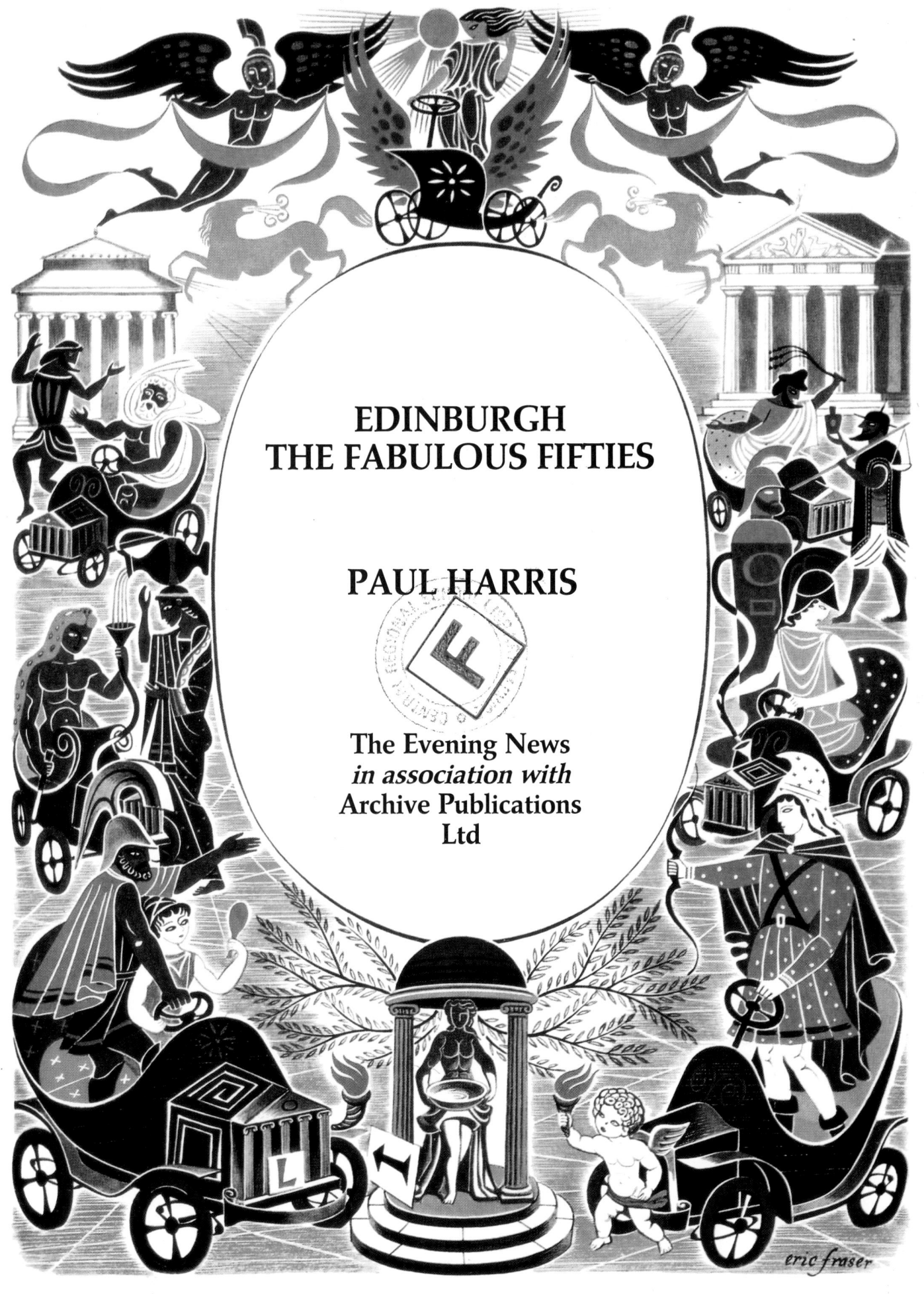

EDINBURGH THE FABULOUS FIFTIES

PAUL HARRIS

The Evening News
in association with
Archive Publications
Ltd

eric fraser

First published 1988 by
The Scotsman Publications Ltd
North Bridge
Edinburgh 1

in association with

Archive Publications Ltd
Carrington Business Park Urmston Manchester

Production by Richardson Press
© Copyright text and arrangement Archive Publications Ltd
Photographs © Copyright The Scotsman Publications Ltd and
contributors
(see Acknowledgements), 1988

ISBN 0 948946 41 5

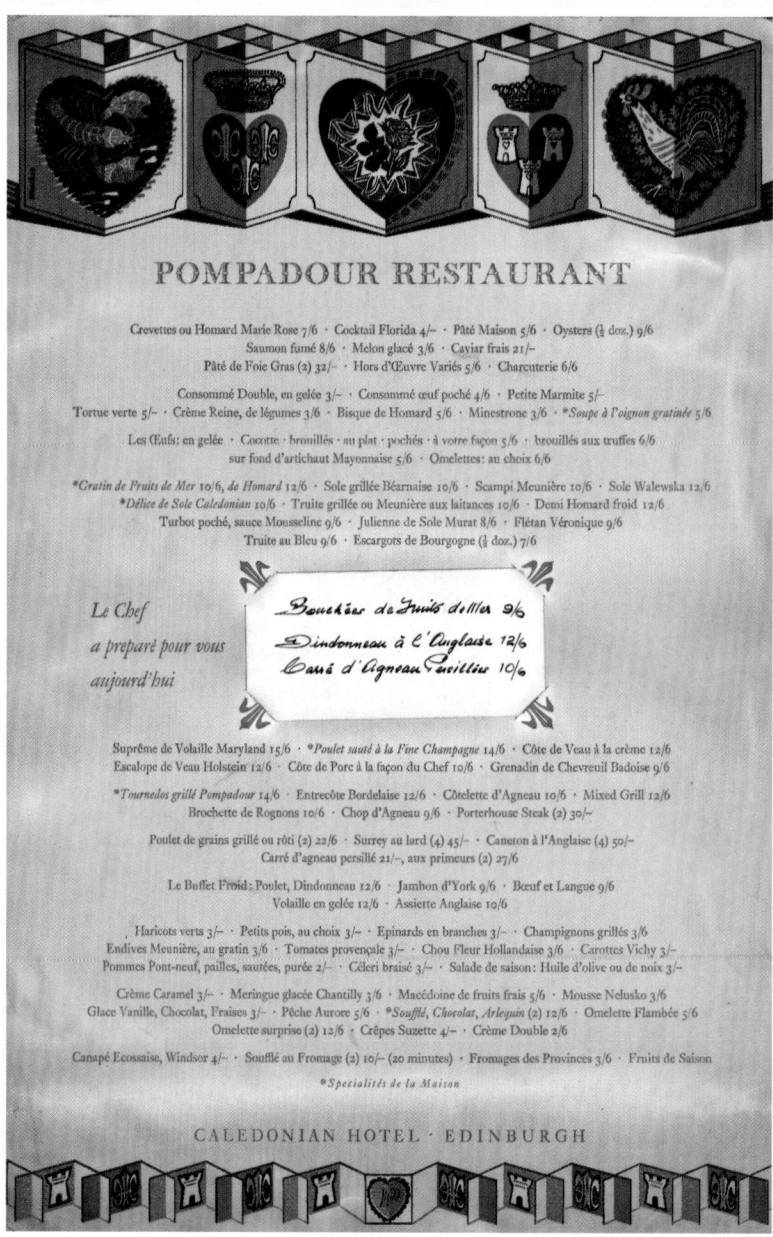

III Stylish menu designed for the Pompadour
Restaurant at the Caledonian Hotel by George
Mackie (1956). Oysters are 9s 6d a dozen —
just over 45 pence!

CONTENTS

INTRODUCTION

FIFTIES CITYSCAPE 1—20

FIFTIES FUN 21—62

FASHION & SHOPPING 63—98

'IT'S GREAT TO BE YOUNG . . .' 99—135

AT WORK 136—158

THERE'S NO BUSINESS LIKE . . . 159—201

TRANSPORT EXPLOSION 202—244

HOLD THE FRONT PAGE! 245—278

ACKNOWLEDGEMENTS

The cooperation, energy and enthusiasm of many people have made this book possible. Effectively a follow-up to *Edinburgh Since 1900*, also published together with The Scotsman Publications Ltd., I am grateful to the staff there who have assisted with this project: to Ranald Allan and Andrew Harton for their support and enthusiasm; to Bill Brady for his unstinting cooperation and hard work in the printing of the glass plates which form the basis of this book; to the staff in the Photo Sales Department and to journalists who assisted me with their recollections and the gathering of information; to Brenda Woods and other staff members in the Library.

Thank you also to Norfolk Capital Hotels PLC and the marketing department at the Caledonian Hotel; to the Publicity Department at Jenners of Princes Street; Alastair Robertson; Victor Robertson and Alastair Clark.

And to everyone else who confirmed — or remedied — my own somewhat hazy recollections of the Fifties.

Reproductions of book, magazine and record covers in the Introduction are from my own collection.

Paul Harris
August 1988

INTRODUCTION

IV Special Souvenir Coronation Number of *Picture Post*, June 13 1953. The Coronation of a new Queen was regarded as a symbol of the hopes for the future.

era, a series of years reckoned from a particular point

(Chambers Twentieth Century Dictionary)

Like any other era in history, the Fifties really cannot be regarded as starting on January 1 1950 and finishing on December 31 1959. There are many singular characteristics of life at that time but, just like the Naughty Nineties, the Swinging Sixties, the Roaring Twenties or the Hungry Forties, as an era the Fifties do not actually neatly fit into the decade. Rather, it seems to me, the Fifties, and all that typifies it, most probably starts with the Festival of Britain in 1951 and the return of the Conservatives to power. It ends somewhere around 1963 with the Beatles, the satire industry, the Wilson election victory of 1964 and the whole new atmosphere of liberality which might be said, in turn, to characterise the Sixties as an era.

The 1950s was a revolutionary era born directly out of the rigours of post-war austerity. After a decade of self denial, consumerism came back for a weary generation starved of fashion, design, entertainment and good living.

With the Festival of Britain, a new Queen and the symbolic scaling of Everest came a new optimism, with all its hope and promise for the future. For a newly liberated generation the Fifties were truly fabulous.

If the Sixties swung, the Twenties Roared and the Nineties and the Forties were marked, respectively, by a passion for vicarious tastes and by empty stomachs, were the Fifties really so fabulous? Looking back on them, and seen in isolation, they probably don't appear so wonderful but there was a certain elemental simplicity, a lack of complication and a directness, exemplified in the words of Bill Haley's explosive 1956 hit:

One, two, three o'clock, four o'clock rock.
Five, six, seven o'clock, eight o'clock rock,
Nine, ten, eleven o'clock, twelve o'clock rock,
We're going to rock
Around
The clock tonight . . .

And it was all so devastatingly original in 1956 . . .

To the teenagers of the time it was a siren call to action. Cinemas screening the film in which the song featured — *The Blackboard Jungle* — hastily pulled it from the screens as

V Souvenir issue of *Illustrated*, June 13 1953.

youngsters leapt to their feet and danced in the aisles. True, some of them ripped out the seats in the cinema but, after all, that was only to make more room for the dancing . . . . Rock 'n' Roll had arrived and with it a youthful rebellion hitherto unknown. The song itself stayed at the top of the charts for almost six months and proved an inspiration to a generation wishing to wash its hands of the crooners and balladeers of its parents. Out of Haley's black-derived music sprang a whole youth culture of coffee bars, Gaggia espresso steam and jukeboxes.

His devastating new influence was more professional and effective than the essentially amateurish skiffle of Chris Barber's 'retired' banjo player, Lonnie Donegan. Skiffle had really been for amateurs able to construct some sort of bass guitar from an old tea chest, a broom handle and some string. But for many inexperienced youngsters it was the way into what was to become a burgeoning pop music industry: way up in Liverpool four young lads were already shaping their own instruments . . .

Soon other British youngsters appeared to make their contribution to what was now developing into a full-blown homegrown popular music industry rapidly replacing the vacuum filled by American artists: Tommy Steele (*aka* Tommy Hicks), Marty Wilde (Reg

VII Cover of *Scottish Field*, April 1954. A classic 50s cover by John Mackay, still well known to readers of the *Evening News*.

Smith), Adam Faith (Terry Nelhams) and Cliff Richard (Harry Webb). Many are still with us today by way of proof of their durability . . . British leadership of the international pop music industry had been firmly established by the end of the 50s.

By the mid '50s there were in Britain some 5 million teenagers and a new word had been found — 'consumer'. All these youngsters were potential consumers of everything from Coca Cola and records to fluorescent socks, cigarettes and, even, by the end of the decade, motor cars.

Neither was the culture of rebellion limited to working class kids. The Saturday night *Six Five Special* spread the word onwards and upwards through the social scale and middle class kids joined the fun. For poor little rich girls, the ultimate rebellion was to run away for love and there was a succession of elopement 'scandals' with Isobel Patino running off to Edinburgh with Jimmy Goldsmith and Tessa Kennedy disappearing off to the West Indies with Dominic Elwes. Things had still not changed sufficiently though for it not to be thought infra dig for an irate father to pursue the fellow involved in order to horsewhip him. But the fact remained that for the first time in British history the social classes were beginning to mix and merge in a manner quite

VI King's Theatre programme, 1959. Cover by J G Rennie.

sewage works supervisor, created the ambitious clerk Joe Lampton in *Room At the Top*. Alan Sillitoe, a Nottingham bicycle factory worker, unleashed his own version of a bicycle worker in the form of Arthur Seaton in *Saturday Night and Sunday Morning*. Not as angry or influential, perhaps, but Keith Waterhouse in *Billy Liar* and Amis in *That Uncertain Feeling* both pursued the general theme of examining the lives of ordinary working class heroes from the ground floor, so to speak. Class barriers were construed as obstacles to be torn down and the assumed resentment from which this stemmed was much discussed. Amidst all this brouhaha, Colin Wilson bicycled along with the largely incomprehensible work *The Outsiders*, written by him while bivouacked on Hampstead Heath, and the press found in the polo-necked philosopher a real life Angry Young Man. The critics loved him. Philip Toynbee of *The Observer* pronounced his ouevre "luminously intelligent . . . truly astounding". The press loved him even more when he ran off with a girl he had not yet married — the permissive society having not yet arrived — and they were pursued

VIII This series of covers for the Edinburgh International Festival Programme during the 50s illustrates the development of design concepts. Above: 1950 Programme.

inconceivable prior to the Second War. Thus the ex-Deb-of-the-Year in Colin MacInnes's *Absolute Beginners* "climbs on the needle when being beautiful is just too much for her".

As the decade progressed, efforts were made by a disparate group of young men to rationalise and intellectualise the far reaching changes occurring within British society. The writers who emerged — often somewhat misleadingly lumped together under the banner of 'The Angry Young Men' — were all drawn from quite different backgrounds to their predecessors in the 30s or 40s. Kingsley Amis — who detested being associated with the others but who, nevertheless, fits the pattern — was the son of a clerk who wrote about an ex-Grammar school boy become disaffected junior university lecturer in *Lucky Jim*. John Osborne, expelled from a minor public school for punching the head, created university dropout Jimmy Porter in *Look Back in Anger*. John Braine, grammar school educated son of a

IX The design is still traditional for the 1952 Programme.

to London by her father brandishing the obligatory horsewhip. The dramatic contretemps which resulted was reported in detail, in words and pictures, in the press the next day — complete with the immortal line from hopelessly outmanouevred father, "The game is up Wilson! We know what's in your filthy diary!"

There were strong elements of social revolution around: a feeling that things were changing in a way they never had before. Indeed they were — but this was not a purely British phenomenon. The publication in France in 1954 of *Bonjour Tristesse* had caused a furore and the young teenage Francois Sagan's novel had been regarded as immoral and scandalous. Fellini's *I Vitelloni* was a cautionary tale of what happened to bored teenagers in a small town and in 1955 Marlon Brando came along as the leader of a group of motorcycle hoodlums terrorising a small American town in the classic film, *The Wild Ones*. And the to-become-legendary James Dean was becoming the star of *Rebel Without a Cause*. It is easy to look at Britain in isolation but, in fact,

XI Artist designed covers have been introduced and the 1955 cover is by Edinburgh artist R Henderson Blyth.

X 1959 cover by Robin Philipson, A.R.S.A.

there were powerful, international forces at work which, as the 50s went on, were brought together by the newly discovered power of television and communications.

Challenging new ideas were abroad and not just from the revolutionary Angry Young Men. In October 1955, Malcolm Muggeridge wrote in the *New Statesman* what was a remarkably provocative and unprecedented article for the time:

"There are probably quite a lot of people — more than might be supposed — who, like myself, feel that another newspaper photograph of the Royal Family will be more than they can bear. — the whole show is utterly out of hand, and there is a much greater danger than might superficially appear that a strong reaction against it might be produced . . ."

This was probably the strongest expression of criticism of the Royals since the Victorian satirists took up cudgels against the Queen's relationship with John Brown and it was symptomatic of the beginning of the breakup of traditional concepts of order in society. In the

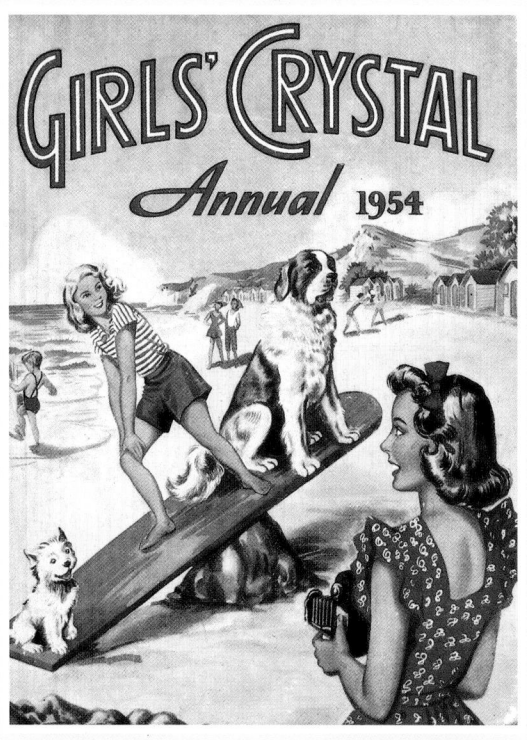

XII All good clean fun. Cover to the *Girls' Crystal Annual* for 1954.

motorway was still to be built. Between 1956 and 1959 Britain's hire purchase debt rose more quickly and by a greater amount overall than at any time in the country's history. Yet there was not a glimmer of understanding of the social implications of domestic debt. But in 1958 you could have become the owner of a brand new Ford Popular for a down payment of just £4 8s 5d. The impact of television had served to broaden the horizons of viewers far beyond their own backyards and workplace. And, naturally, the advertising industry had grasped this new opportunity with a unique fervour.

Until the introduction of commercial television in 1955, the BBC had ruled the roost and maintained its own very individual standards. Television was not yet the all pervasive medium which it was shortly to become: the biggest single provider of leisure activity in Britain. A glimpse of the power and potential of the medium had been afforded in 1953 when the Coronation was broadcast to the country live from London. At the time, this was a mindbending experience for millions of

same year T R Fyvel encapsulated what was happening in the magazine *Encounter:*

"It is ruling classes which set cultural patterns and for more than a century the dominant culture of Europe has been that of the well-to-do middle classes, the haute bourgeoisie. It was a culture that went with those great English social inventions: the Gentlemen's club . . . amateur sport and the long weekend . . . In all its aspects . . . this bourgeois way of life was also a minority culture from which the lower class majority of the population was . . . excluded. It is this bourgeois minority culture . . . that has been crumbling. What we are now entering instead is a social era based on mass-participation."

All these complex forces of change, economic and social, had come together at a time of rapid technological advance and all were, in turn, being intellectualised by a new generation of writers and thinkers. A more socially explosive package would be difficult to visualise.

Some of these changes were happening so fast that one gets the feeling that any sort of central control or direction had been lost. Between 1949 and 1964 the number of cars on Britain's roads increased tenfold. Yet the first

XIII Uncle Mac's radio *Childrens' Hour* was a Saturday morning institution in the 50s.

people who gathered around flickering black and white television sets wherever they could be found. Could all this really be going on as we watch it now? Virtually everybody alive who was old enough to look at a TV screen in 1953 can remember the broadcasting of the Coronation just as people seem to be able to remember exactly where they were when Kennedy was shot. Once every few decades there occurs an event which impinges itself upon the general consciousness in such a way that it is never eradicated.

Independent television, by and large, inflicted a fairly unedifying diet upon an unsophisticated audience. The first week of broadcasts brought *I Love Lucy, Dragnet, Double Your Money, Take Your Pick* and *Opportunity Knocks* into the living rooms of Britain. The commercials were far from the polished, subliminal efforts of today. But they were very effective and the viewing audience seemed to accept unquestionably such assurances as, "Omo improves even on perfect whiteness". The popularity of this fare was borne out not only by the viewing figures — in short order the BBC share of the audience sank to around 30 % of viewers — but also by the longevity of many of the shows. *Double Your Money* and *Opportunity Knocks*, hosted by the bland and smarmy Hughie Green, both lasted around 20 years. This is not to suggest that the

VOL XXXVIII No 10   OCTOBER 1953

MECCANO MAGAZINE

APOLLO AT CREWE

XV As technical developments raced on in the 50s many magazines catered to the hunger for knowledge which was a feature of the time. The *Meccano Magazine* was one of the most popular.

BBC did not have many hugely successful shows, well presented and featuring some of the best known personalities of the 50s. A case in point was the popular game show *What's My Line?* with Eamonn Andrews in the chair and featuring Lady Isobel Barnett, David Nixon, Gilbert Harding and Barbara Kelly. All enjoyed long careers and were worshipped by their audiences. If you made it on television in the 50s you really had set yourself up on a pedestal from which it was almost impossible to be toppled.

One of the more unfortunate observations of the 50s came from Canadian Roy Thomson, owner of The Scotsman Publications and founder of Scottish Television, when he opined that a television licence was "a licence to print money". In fact, when he had tried to raise the cash to start STV in 1957 he could only raise less than a quarter of the money required (which itself was less than half a million pounds) from the canny Scots. Although a little hard up at the time, Sir Compton Mackenzie sent him off a tenner. It was a good investment. When the company went public the share value had multiplied twenty two times. Thomson commented, "It is ironic now to think of the money those men, some of them shrewd in

100mph!

The new Daimler 3½ litre One-O-Four

XIV This really was the last word in motoring at the 1955 Motor Show.

XVI A typical late 50s living room scene is depicted on this record cover.

XVII Lovestruck 50s Miss

XVIII Watercolour of The Royal Scottish Academy and Princes Street by Robert Eadie, painted in 1949.

business, could have made." A bawbee saved was not a bawbee made, in this instance.

The diet of imported American series which appeared on commercial television directly fed the consumer revolution. Series like *I Love Lucy* showed homes stuffed with fitted kitchens, fridges, freezers, pop up toasters, food mixers and with cars in the drive. Things were not like that over here . . . at least not until the end of the decade.

Whilst a hunger developed for all things new, bright and wonderful there existed, beneath a thin veneer of newly acquired sang froid, an uncertainty and childlike naivety; of awe generated by a whole series of inventions, innovations and technical developments, each more incomprehensible than the last. It was a

XX Two items from the Jenners Christmas Catalogue for 1959. A 'flattering' cocktail hat with "a whisper of black veiling with feathery fronds and diamante spots".

XIX Model with French satin ribbon scarf.

XXI Call it what you like — religious fervour or plain hype — the 1955 visit by American evangelist Billy Graham to Scotland was, for its time, a consumately handled media event with, even, a Graham tartan-covered song book.

favourite tale, in Rose Street's Abbotsford bar in the early 60s, of the American academic who had come to Scotland to meet Hugh MacDiarmid, poet and subject of his doctoral thesis. Alas for the groves of academe, the week of the Abbotsford meeting the Great Man had bought his first drip-dry shirt and MacDiarmid talked incessantly of this new wonder to the complete bafflement of the transatlantic researcher.

With baffling speed, the age of jet travel was followed by the age of atomic energy which in turn was superceded, in terms of wonderment, by the Sputnik. And all this for a generation which had already been bemused by everyday objects from polyfilla and bubble cars to motorways and a vast bridge across the Forth. Just like MacInnes's hero at the airport. "I got a Coke and went and gazed, and it certainly was a sight! All those aircraft landing from outer

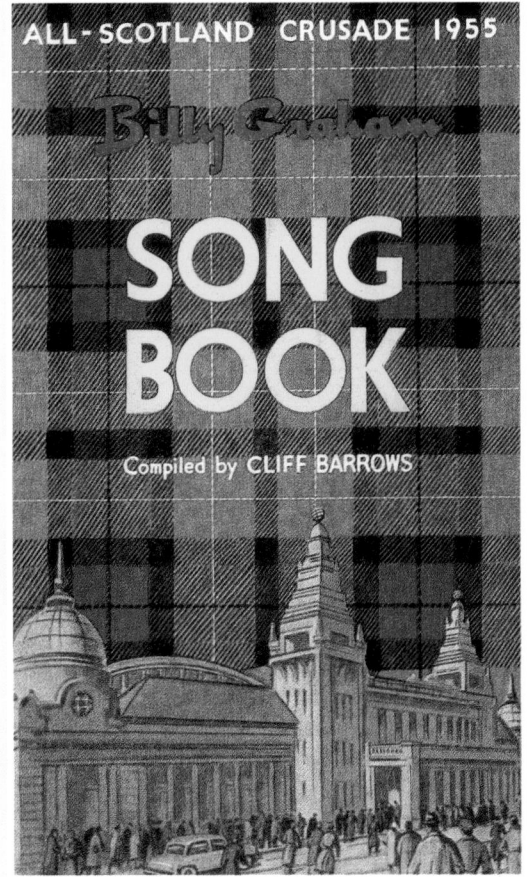

ALL-SCOTLAND CRUSADE 1955

Billy Graham's

SONG BOOK

Compiled by CLIFF BARROWS

space, and taking off to all the nations of the world! And I thought to myself, standing there looking out on all this fable — what an age it is I've grown up in, with everything possible to mankind at last . . .".

XXII *Picture Post* was one of the most popular magazines of the 50s although by 1955 its brand of photojournalism was coming under attack from television.

XXIII Advertisement for Morris family cars, 1955.

XXIV The designer of this 50s showcard had obviously discovered the selling power of a pretty girl — even in the marketing of something as mundane as baler twine.

RECOMMENDED FURTHER READING

As yet, the 1950s have not been covered quite as exhaustively as other decades of this century. The best sources to get a real flavour of the period remain the newspapers and magazines: *The Scotsman, The Evening News, The Evening Dispatch, The Weekly Scotsman, Vogue, Picture Post, Scottish Field* and *Scotland's SMT* magazine.

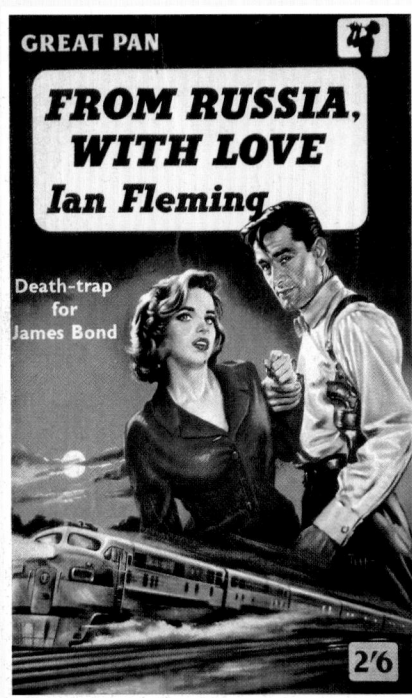

XXV James Bond was very much a product of the 50s. The first Bond book to be published was *Casino Royale* (1953) and this new jet set hero held enormous appeal for a society with expanding horizons. Cover for Pan edition of *From Russia with Love* (1959).

The Edinburgh Year Book, 1955, 1956.

There are interesting general surveys of the period in the following books:
Christopher Booker: *The Neophiliacs*, London 1969.
Nicholas Drake: *The Fifties in Vogue*, London 1987.
Peter Lewis: *The Fifties*, London 1978.
Arthur Marwick: *British Society since 1945*, London 1982.
Anthony Sampson: *Anatomy of Britain*, London 1962.

More specific aspects of life in the 50s are dealt with in these books:
D Elliston Allen: *British Tastes*, London 1968
George Bruce: *Festival in the North*, London 1975
T R Fyvel: *The Insecure Offenders*, London 1961
Jim Haynes: *Thanks for Coming!*, London 1984
Ann Lloyd (ed.): *Movies of the Fifties*, London 1982
Mary Morse: *The Unattached*, London 1965
Hugh Thomas (ed.): *The Establishment*, London 1959
Colin Wilson: *The Outsiders*, London 1956

The best novel of Edinburgh life this century remains *The Black Oxen* by Bruce Marshall (London 1972). A more general picture can be gained from:
Kingsley Amis: *Lucky Jim*, London, 1954
John Braine: *Room at the Top*, London 1957
Colin MacInnes: *Absolute Beginners*, London 1959
Alan Sillitoe: *Saturday Night and Sunday Morning*, London 1958
Keith Waterhouse: *Billy Liar*, London 1959

XXVII This classically understated cover (1959) for the first British edition of *Lolita* belied its explosive contents which caused a sensation when it was discovered the book was concerned with the infatuation of an older man with a 12 year-old girl.

XXVI Feeding young minds

FIFTIES CITYSCAPE

1.   Floral Clock on the Mound for The Festival of Britain, 1951.

The Fifties really start with the Festival of Britain in 1951 and although Edinburgh was far removed from the remarkable exhibition mounted on the Embankment in London the general atmosphere of hope and optimism was keenly felt (1). As photographs of the centre of the city in the early 50s indicate, there were comparatively few private cars (2, 3, 4, 5) and, indeed, in the whole of Britain in 1950 there were, as yet, only 1 million vehicles. Public transport — and the tram in particular — is the way in which most people go to work. The New Town (8, 9, 10) still looks much as it must have been in Georgian times — if one mentally substitutes a horse and carriage for the odd horseless carriage which is to be seen. The ease of shopping in areas outside the centre now clogged with traffic, is notable (11, 12, 13) and the ball and chain of the demolition men has yet to assault some well known landmarks (15, 16, 17). For the moment life goes on very much as it did before the war and it is the late 50s and early 60s which really begin to see physical changes in the appearance of the City.

2.   Edinburgh from The Mound, 1955.

3.   Laying new cables into the Head Post office at the east end of Princes Street in July 1952. As yet, there is little evidence of the approaching revolution in personal transport: the tram still reigns supreme.

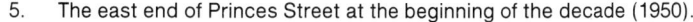

4. A no. 23 tramcar in Hanover Street beside the statue of King George IV, November 1956. Motor cars are parked nose-in to the kerb.

5. The east end of Princes Street at the beginning of the decade (1950).

REMOVALS
Binns
EDINBURGH
REMOVALS
STORAGE
PRINCES ST.
EDINBURGH
KEEP LEFT
OVALTINE
GREYS

BINNS LTD
BINNS
LIMITED
BINNS LTD
BINNS LTD

Randolph Crescent in the early '50s. At that time there was a plan to build in the gardens of the Crescent which, for a while, seemed certain to go ahead despite local opposition. In 1955 it was proposed that a car park should be built in Princes Street Gardens, which plan, fortunately, also came to nothing.

A startling innovation at the time, the new experimental traffic roundabout at Haymarket (December 1954).

Binns Corner, March 1953. Travellers wait on the island in the middle of the street for their tram home.

Circus Gardens, 1953. The iron railings were removed in the war along with so many others in a misguided, though psychologically successful, salvage scheme promoted by wartime government. In practice the iron railings were quite unsuitable for the building of guns and batttleships. It is only comparatively recently that the Circus Gardens railings were replaced.

10. St. Vincent Place, 1950, with St. Stephen's Church beyond. The number of New Town motor car owners is, as yet, insignificant.

11. Shopping in Morningside.

12. Stockbridge, 1954.

13. Shopping in Gorgie.

14. Snow at the foot of Lothian Road, February 1955.

15. Leith Street in the 1950s before the St. James' development. It was an attractive street with shopping on two levels rather in the continental style.

16. The old Kirkgate, Leith, before the present modern shopping development.

17. The Kirkgate, Leith. It is July 1957 and the FOR SALE placard is up on the Gaiety Theatre.

18. The Shore at Leith in the early 50s — long before the birth of the modern Yuppie. Fishing yawls are beached at The Shore at what is now known as the King's Landing (although King George IV actually steppped ashore for his celebrated visit directly opposite). Modern, luxury housing now stands at the point from which this atmospheric photograph is taken. Twenty yards or so upstream was the Bernard Street swing bridge. On April 25 1955 the swing bridge swung for the last time and this stetch of the Water of Leith was closed to navigation. On the other side of the water, at the end of the block, are two old Leith bars. The Imperial is now the fashionable Shore Bar and restaurant.

19. Once a popular feature of the Meadows, the bandstand, photographed in 1949 before its demolition.

20. A platform policeman at the East end of Princes Street (1956).

FIFTIES FUN

21.   In the heyday of its popularity, Portobello Beach crowded by trades holidaymakers, July 1952.

In the Fifties Edinburgh still enjoyed a very considerable manufacturing base with many large industrial works. Trades Fortnight in July, accordingly, was holiday time for the vast majority of workers. This was the age before the Spanish holiday and many people holidayed near to home — it wasn't possible to holiday much nearer than Portobello but it was still a very popular resort in the 50s (21, 22, 29).

It was a time of 'crazes', of filmgoing and 'the dancing' for, as yet, television had not permeated society in the way it was to in the 60s. The hula-hoop (33—4) took the whole country by storm. All types of dancing flourished from old time (44) to the then modern jive (52—3) and rock'n'roll (56). Many youngsters went to the dancing most nights of the week (54—5) and sartorial elegance — of a sort — made a comeback in the 50s (51). Sexism was an unknown and totally alien concept in an age when gentlemen really did prefer blondes — as exemplified in the Mazda Queen of Light Competition (47) and beauty competitions generally were a regular feature of life for the better looking — or vainer — 'chicks' (45—6).

Some of the more traditional aspects of life carried on much as before, like the Royal Garden Party at Holyrood although the year 1958 brought a small indication of changing times when the Palace indicated that it would be the last year that 'debs' would be presented (39), thus finally bringing to an end a tradition which had been in force since 1786. The glittering social events that had almost become mini-constellations within the orbit of the annual Royal visit were now also under attack (40) in an altogether more egalitarian and meritocratic atmosphere. Along with sexism, the idea of animal rights was still light years away and for youngsters a visit to the circus was one of the most exciting things in the world (41—2).

Up until 1911, John Henry Cooke had provided a resident circus for the citizens of Edinburgh. Latterly, he had operated from a large building in Fountainbridge (later to become the Palladium Theatre) and after his demise Mr A F Lumley, who took over the lease of the Waverley Market, in 1913, provided circus entertainment during the festive season.

Even those who could not afford the luxury of a visit to the Big Top (or Waverley Market) could share in the atmosphere and experience simply watching from the kerbside in Princes Street as the Parade went by (43).

22. "Watch the birdie!" Trades holidaymakers snapped at Portobello, July 1958.

23. "All aboard the *Skylark*" in this holiday scene at Portobello, July 1957. There is plenty of action on the beach with donkey rides, deckchairs and swimming. The prevalence of overcoats, however, would seem to indicate that the weather was not all it might have been . . .

4. Trades Fortnight and
   holidaymakers queue
   at Waverley Station,
   July 4 1959.

5. Holiday queue for the
   ferry to Fife at South
   Queensferry, April 1955.

26. Elephant rides at the zoo for Edinburgh Spring holidaymakers, April 1955. It cost just 6d. in old money for a ride on Sally.

27. Holiday crowds at Cramond, August 1958.

28. The Edinburgh taxi drivers' childrens outing has been a regular June event since the 1950s. Here, in 1958, Mr. D Reid is congratulated by former Chief Constable William Merrilees as driver of the 'gayest' taxi in the days before the word became monopolised in another context.

29. More holiday queues — this time for the open air swimming pool at Portobello, June 1957.

30. Dumbo the baby elephant at the zoo, August 1958.

31. Yachting regatta at Cramond.

32. At Woodhouses' staff dance in the Edinburgh Room at the Assembly Rooms, local model and beauty queen May Liddell demonstrates the hula hoop. It was a lot more difficult than it looked!

33. In November 1958 the hula hoop craze was at its height. Here a consignment of 2,500 of them arrive at Waverley Station. A British Rail spokesman commented, at the time, that this was "a typical daily delivery" during that month.

Queueing seems to have been a regular feature of life in the 1950s. Here patrons are waiting to to get into the Embassy Cinema, Pilton, to see *Bridge on the River Kwai* (1957).

35. A special matinee for four-legged friends. Dogs (and owners) enter the Regal Cinema in Lothian Road to see *Old Yeller* (June 1958), Walt Disney's best film about a boy and his dog on a farm in Texas in the 1850s. The all star cast included Fess Parker, famous in the 50s as Davy Crockett.

36. By the end of the 50s screens were closing. Here the furnishings are auctioned off at the Alhambra Cinema in Leith Walk (August 1959).

37. A July 1957 view of Musselburgh Races serves as a reminder that, at that time, all off course betting was still illegal, and the bookies' stances are doing a roaring trade. The law was changed in 1961 and bookies' shops became a feature on the high street.

38. A 1954 view of stock car racing at Meadowbank — a Vauxhall in the foreground.

39. The Royal Garden Party at Holyrood is, of course, an old established institution but this is a feature of it which has been allowed to die out. This photograph was taken in July 1958 prior to the last presentation party for Scottish debutantes: this was 'the last curtsy' for Scottish socialites, although there was just one more presentation of debs at Buckingham Palace. Some 750 debs and their sponsors were at Holyrood.

40. Many upper crust social events took place within the orbit of the Royal visit at the beginning of July. Here are some programme sellers at the charity Victoria League Ball at the Assembly Rooms, 1958.

41. The circus comes to town. In the 1950s circuses regularly appeared in the old Waverley Market.

43. Camels in the Chipperfields' Circus Parade, Princes Street, 1955. The Parade was a popular precursor to performances underneath the Big Top.

42. The Bertram Mills 'flying elephant', June 1956.

44. Old time dancing, the new Cavendish Ballroom, 1954.

45. The Palais de Danse Beauty Competition, May 1960. Edinburgh 'Queen of Beauty' Elizabeth Anderson with runner up May Liddle.

46. Finalists in the Palais de Danse Miss Lambretta competition (1958). The Lambretta scooter was a powerful symbol of style in the 50s.

47. The Edinburgh final of the Mazda Queen of Light Competition, October 1958. This competition was open to blondes only and it is recorded that the winner was a Mrs Zena Balls.

48. The Edinburgh area finalists in the Post Office Personality Girls Contest (1959). Left to right: Margaret Sinclair, Moira Cunningham, Jean Arnott, Georgina Logan, Yvonne Howarth, Sheila Rugg, Nancy Armstrong, Catherine Browne, Margaret Watson, Helen Wright. A trip to America was the unbelievable prize!

49. An expert panel of judges at a Palais de Danse beauty competition (1959).

50. The three finalists.

51. The dress of a typical 17-year-old in the late 50s. Alex McFarlane's preferred dress consisted of a black and white striped jacket, black 'Maverick' waistcoat (named after the popular TV Western series), blue trousers, black suede crepes, red open neck shirt, sloppy joe and medallion. "I call myself the average Ted," he opined. "We've nothing against squares. We'd never dress like them but we've learned to put up with them."

52. Jiving champions, 1962.

53. Jiving competition, 1958.

54. A view of the newly refurbished Palais de Danse, November 1958, at a party night to mark Mecca's 21st Birthday at the Palais in Fountainbridge. The Palais was constructed out of the back of the Picturehouse and in 1956 the cinema was converted into an entrance hall for the Palais — the largest in Britain. At that time there were 60 staff and resident band leader was Harry Roy. The dancing was non-stop (a novelty for the time) which was facilitated by a revolving stage which brought the next band around immediately. In 1957 a new dance floor was installed, built on springs.

55. Patrons remember the Palais as a particularly well run dance hall. The 'cocktail bar', Cupids Corner, served fruit juice cocktails only. On Wednesday nights there was old time dancing for OAPs who got in free.

56. Rock 'n' Roll at the Palais. A demonstration by Johnny Wilson's Sinners, a formation team from Glasgow who appeared on TV at the time.

57.   This 1958 picture was, apparently, typical of "teenagers with nothing to do." Especially on Sundays, they used to gather at the foot of The Mound where this group was photographed. Church youth clubs attempted, so far as possible, to entertain such apparently aimless individuals but it was seen as a real problem at the time.

58.   Hearts F C reception after their 1959 League Cup win. Mackay, Murray, Bauld and Crawford with the Cup.

59.   Skaters on the Union Canal at Craiglockhart, February 1956.

60.   Hearts players train at Tynecastle, July 1959.

61.   Hearts v. Rangers at Tynecastle, March 19 1956. Willie Bauld scores.

62. Hearts dinner at the Grosvenor Hotel, December 1952. Left to right: Wardhaugh, Conn, Mackenzie, Bauld, Armstrong, McLaren, Wilson, Jamieson, Campbell.

FASHION & SHOPPING

The photograph renders changes in fashion and shopping immediately obvious. Most of the old department stores have fallen victim to a wave of revolutions in retailing and names like Forsyths (70), Patrick Thomsons (67—8) and Smalls (64) have gone for ever: only Jenners now remains of the grand old stores (65—6).

One cannot help thinking that shopping was both a more social and leisurely activity in the 50s. Demonstrations of exciting new gadgets and commercial products were a regular feature, particularly in the larger shops (77—9) and every whim of fashion was reflected in one or another of the mannequin parades so popular at the time (83—7, 89). The fashion scene was still dominated by the traditional 'Classical' look which was largely a recycling of pre-war designs at the hands of designers like Dior (91) and Hartnell (64). Dior's 'New Look' had been introduced in 1947 and taken up by other designers: it dominated the fashion scene until the mid '50s. Quite apart from the fact that many of the fashions now appear to us as decidedly ludicrous, like the ballon swimsuit (83) and bloomers (84), others are now outmoded by changes in social attitudes. An exhibition of fur hats would guarantee a demonstration today (81) and if in business in Princes Street today, Marcus the Furriers would be forced to adopt a more circumspect image (82).

Social changes were also about to hasten the demise of the old circulating library where books could be borrowed in a section of the bookshop set aside for paid loans of books. The Douglas & Foulis library (74) was a typical example, flourishing up to the early '60s, when the public library system reached its zenith.

The Fifties were marked by a passion for modernising everything in sight. Concepts of design came back for the first time since the Thirties. The Second World War had effectively arrested the development of design concepts for a whole decade and by way of reaction against the formless designs of the war years in came spindly legs on 'contemporary' furniture, flared coffee table tops and fantastic mixtures of colours and textures which seemed to reaffirm for consumers that the age of austerity and drabness had now firmly passed for ever. Unfortunately, this was often exemplified in a quite undiscerning quest for modernisation as any traditional extant features in houses and public places were ripped out, covered up, flushed, tiled and generally ruined by undistinguished and transient design. A couple of wonderful examples of Fifties taste are illustrated in the home cocktail bar (92) and the cocktail bar at the North British Hotel (98), a real gem of its type with spindly stools and chairs, tables reminiscent of flying saucers, sculpted abstract ornamentation and, as a sort of concession to the Georgian antecedents of the locale, stylised coloured panels on doors and where cornices just might have been.

63. The changed face of shopping — all this lot for 30 bob (i. e. £ 1.50) in the mid '50s!

64. Designer Norman Hartnell opens Smalls renovated shop in Princes Street, March 1954.

65. Noel Coward visits Jenners to sign copies of his autobiography *Future Indefinite*.

66. Gracie Fields visits Jenners 'Television Lounge', as it was somewhat quaintly known (1954).

67. The queue for Patrick Thomson's Sale, North Bridge, June 1956.

68. The old Patrick Thomson's store on North Bridge, now reconstructed as shops and the Carlton Highland Hotel.

69. Blyths Sale, Earl Grey Street, Tollcross, July 1958.

70. R & W Forsyth Department Store, Princes Street.

71. *previous bottom right:* Grant's house furnishing department store on North Bridge, now redeveloped into flats (Royal Mile Mansions) with shops and a restaurant at ground floor level. The business started in 1923 in a small shop in the High Street. In 1958 their toy department advertised the latest thing — a toy car driven by batteries. "The domestic and maternal instincts of young girls are well catered for too . . . ."

72. J & R Allan's new Food Hall, December 1954.

73. Christmas shopping in Thornton's book department, 1958.

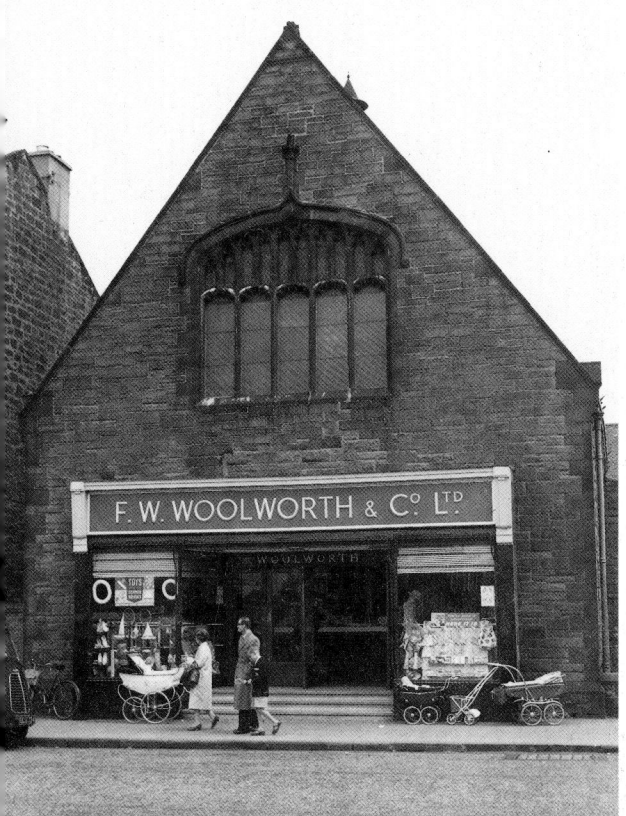

74. The old Douglas & Foulis bookshop in Castle Street. Right up to the end of the 50s lending libraries were a common feature of larger bookshops but as the public lending library service improved the commerical libraries declined.

75. Woolworths store in the church, High Street, Portobello.

76. The new Marks & Spencer store under construction, February 1955.

77. A cookery demonstration in the Usher Hall with Fanny and Johnny Craddock, October 1957.

78. An *Evening Dispatch* housewives' demonstration
     of the BURCO washing machine (1959).

79. Another *Dispatch* sponsored housewives' demonstration, this
     time of Persil washing powder. One assumes housewives were
     incapable of using the stuff under their own steam, so to speak.

80. The milliner, Edward French. In the 50s his well known hat business operated from Princes Street premises. He then moved to George Street and later down to Howe Street, which premises he occupied until he retired in the mid 70s. The 50s was a splendid era for the hat and social occasions were still characterised by the sort of formality which required the head to be fashionably covered.

81. The Edward French Hat Show in George Street, October 1959. The fur hat was in vogue that season.

82. Miss Currie gives the bear the brush off at the Princes Street premises of Marcus, the furriers. The bear was the well known symbol of the shop.

83. Mannequin Parade at Thorntons of Princes Street, Spring 1959. This scarlet silk jersey 'ballon style' swimsuit caused a sensation at the time. "For those not daring enought to wear it in its original shape there are tapes which tie around the waist and drape the swimsuit into Grecian style."

84. At a 1962 Mannequin Parade a member of the Royal Overseas League models Darlings clothes: beach top, hat and bloomer in the latest style.

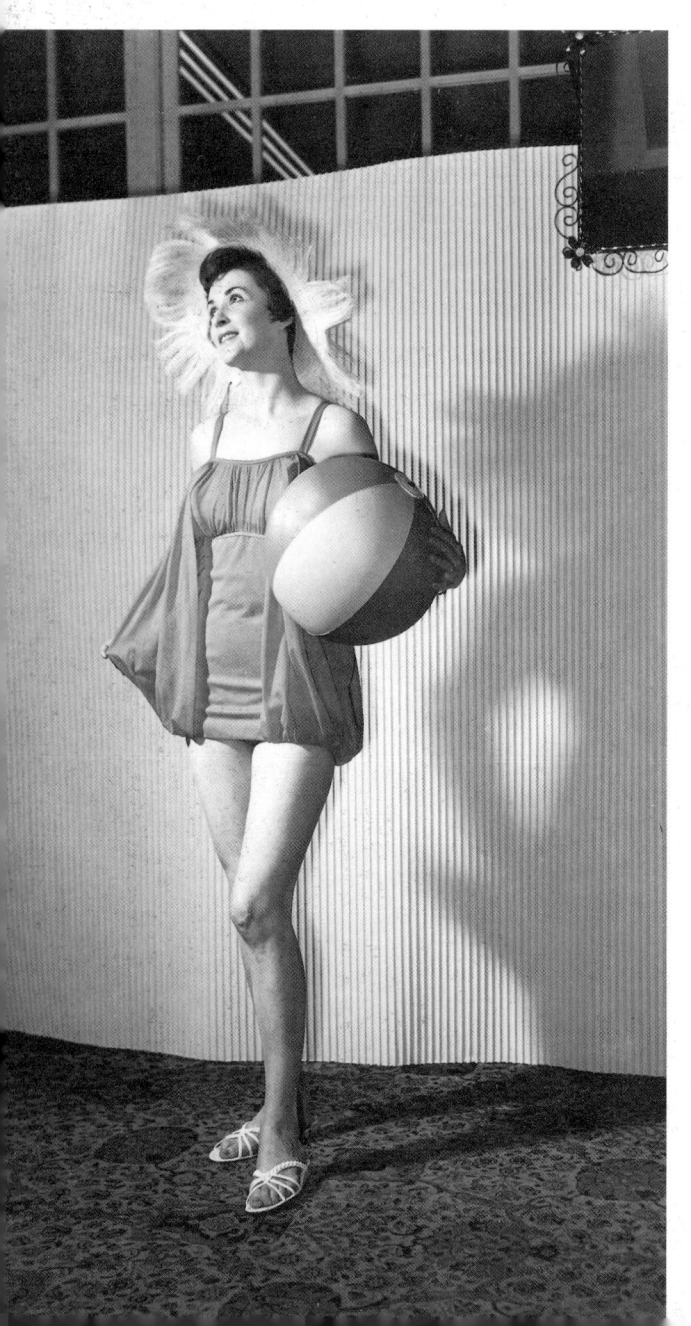

85. More bathing costumes for summer 1958. These were on show at Smalls Mannequin Parade.

86. Patrick Thomsons Mannequin Parade (May 1958).

87. The 1956 Scottish Fashion Festival, predictably, featured tartan. These models were photographed at Edinburgh Castle.

88. The Davy Crockett craze spawned a whole fashion of its own. This 'cool cat' in Princes Street sports not only the genuine racoon skin hat but also a fur coat.

89. Six models from Darlings Mannequin Parade (October 1959).

90. In September 1958, the Jaeger Shop in Princes Street put this vicuna coat on sale at the then incredible price of £180!

91. Christian Dior sightseeing in Edinburgh with his wife in May 1955. Dior died in 1957 shortly after unleashing on the fashion world one of his very few designs which was actually comfortable — the waistless 'Sack'.

92. The latest thing in 1959 — a cocktail bar made of cane manufactured in Hong Kong and ready to instal at home.

94. *bottom right:* Cadburys Chocolate House, Princes Street (1957).

93. The Barbecue Restaurant, Forrest Road (1958). Now 'The Doctors', public house.

95. *top left:* The Carlton Hotel Bar (1958).

96. The Berkeley Restaurant, Lothian Road

97. *left:* Grants new restaurant, North Bridge (1955).

98. The cocktail bar at the North British Hotel (1954).

'IT'S GREAT TO BE YOUNG!'

99.   The end of sweetie rationing in Edinburgh in 1953! Food rationing did not end completely until July 1954.

This was the suggestion, indeed the imprecation, in the 1956 film of the title in which a young and popular teacher led a pupil revolt against a strict new headmaster seeking to disband the school orchestra. The film was extremely popular at the time but has been proved eminently forgettable by history. If it did say anything lastingly meaningful, it did indicate greater indulgence of the young in the Fifties.

For most of the '50s, the sophistication and worldly-wisdom which were to hold sway with children in the television era had not yet arrived. Although during the mid '50s the then wondrous new invention was beginning to appear in an increasingly large number of homes, programmes still tended towards the homespun and hours of viewing were strictly limited. It was not yet the complete window on the world it was to become in the '60s. Traditional pursuits then were still very much to the fore

like the now vanished street games (100—106), playing in the park (107—8) and back green concerts (109). The fantasy world of the typical boy revolved around Wild West characters like Roy Rogers (112), Hopalong Cassidy (113), The Lone Ranger (115) and Davie Crockett (116), who could be viewed at the Saturday morning film clubs (114), noisy and riotous events where audience participation was very much the order of the day. For the younger and more sedate there were the pleasures of the Lee Puppet Theatre (121) or Harry Corbett with Sooty and Sweep (118).

The general attitude towards schooling was generally considerably more reverential than it is today, although social differences are quite pointed, no more so than in the pictures of pupils lunching at Peffermill School (128) and Daniel Stewart's College (129).

100. The 'guider', a home made self-propelled contraption put together from old pram wheels, bits of wood and anything else that happened to be around, was a great source of fun to kids in the 50s. Here some Edinburgh 'guider mechanics' are seen at work (1957).

101. Guiders away in South Fort Street. Kids queue for a 'snottie'.

102. Playing the policeman in South Fort Street, Leith, is local lad Brian Pithie (1957).

103. Rolling Easter eggs in Abercorn Park, Portobello.

104. Skipping games, Lapicide Place, Leith (1957).

105. A 'cuddie' fight in Tron Square (1954).

106. Playing marbles (1955).

107. Down Arthur's Seat on a piece of wood! (1959).

108. Children boating, St. Margaret's Loch, Holyrood Park (April 1956).

109. Childrens' playroom, Jamaica Street (1954).

110. A back green concert in Marchmont in 1959. Patricia and Lynda Walton demonstrate the craze of the time — the hula hoop.

111. Musselburgh Fancy Dress Parade for children, July 1958.

112. Roy Rogers makes his way to his room at the Caledonian Hotel — down the main staircase with his horse Trigger. After the publicity stunt the horse was, in fact, sent off to the Scottish Co-op stables in the city where, there were actually two Triggers stabled. The stage act, apparently, was so demanding that it was a case of one performance per horse daily and so two were required (1954). It is not recorded which of the two was stuffed and thereby immortalised at the Roy Rogers ranch.

113. Another Western hero, Hopalong Cassidy, played by William Boyd, at the Regal (1954). The all-in-black, very much second feature cowboy made his original debut as far back as 1935.

114. The ABC Minor Club at the Lyceum Picture House (1958).

115. Clayton Moore, better known as The Lone Ranger (Hi-ho Silver!), visited Edinburgh in 1958. There was a successful TV series and two feature films with Moore and Jay Silverheels who played his Indian sidekick, Tonto.

116. *bottom right:* The Davie Crockett craze gripped the country in the mid '50s. In the film, Davie Crockett was played by a 6 foot 5 inch real life Texan named Fess Parker, photographed here at Edinburgh Castle with Private Robert Wallace. He is not wearing typical Davie Crockett apparel . . .

"How's this for Davy Crockett, Sarge?"

117. Hairdressing for kids at Patrick Thomsons — not a favourite way to spend a Saturday morning but the entertainments helped!

118. Sooty, the incorrigible glove puppet, and his owner and 'victim' Harry Corbett (1955).

119. *opposite top:* Christmas shopping in Thornton's toy department (1958).

120. *opposite below left:* Miniature doggy person Miss Brown and her Boxer at the dog show in Waverley Market in 1958.

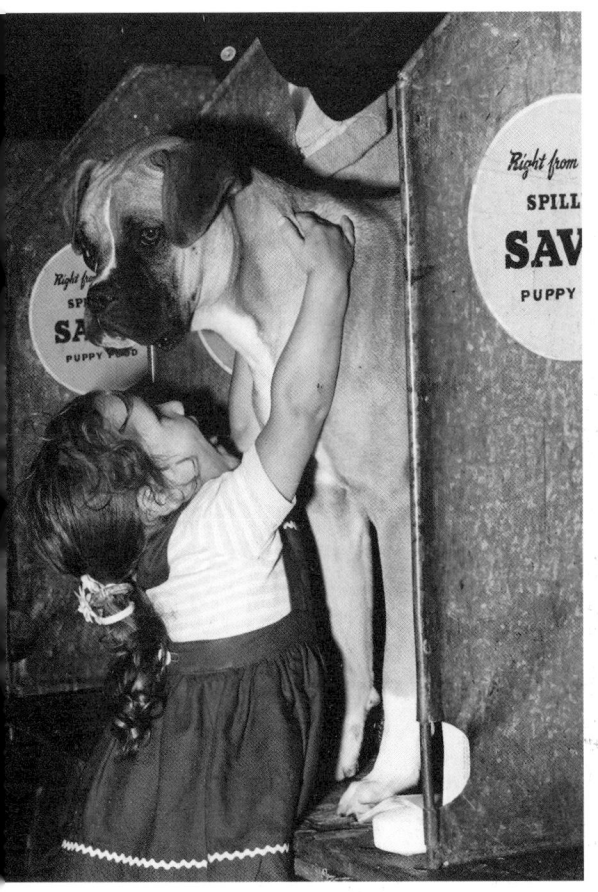

121. The Lee Puppet Theatre, Belgrave Mews, and a source of wonder for many 50s children.

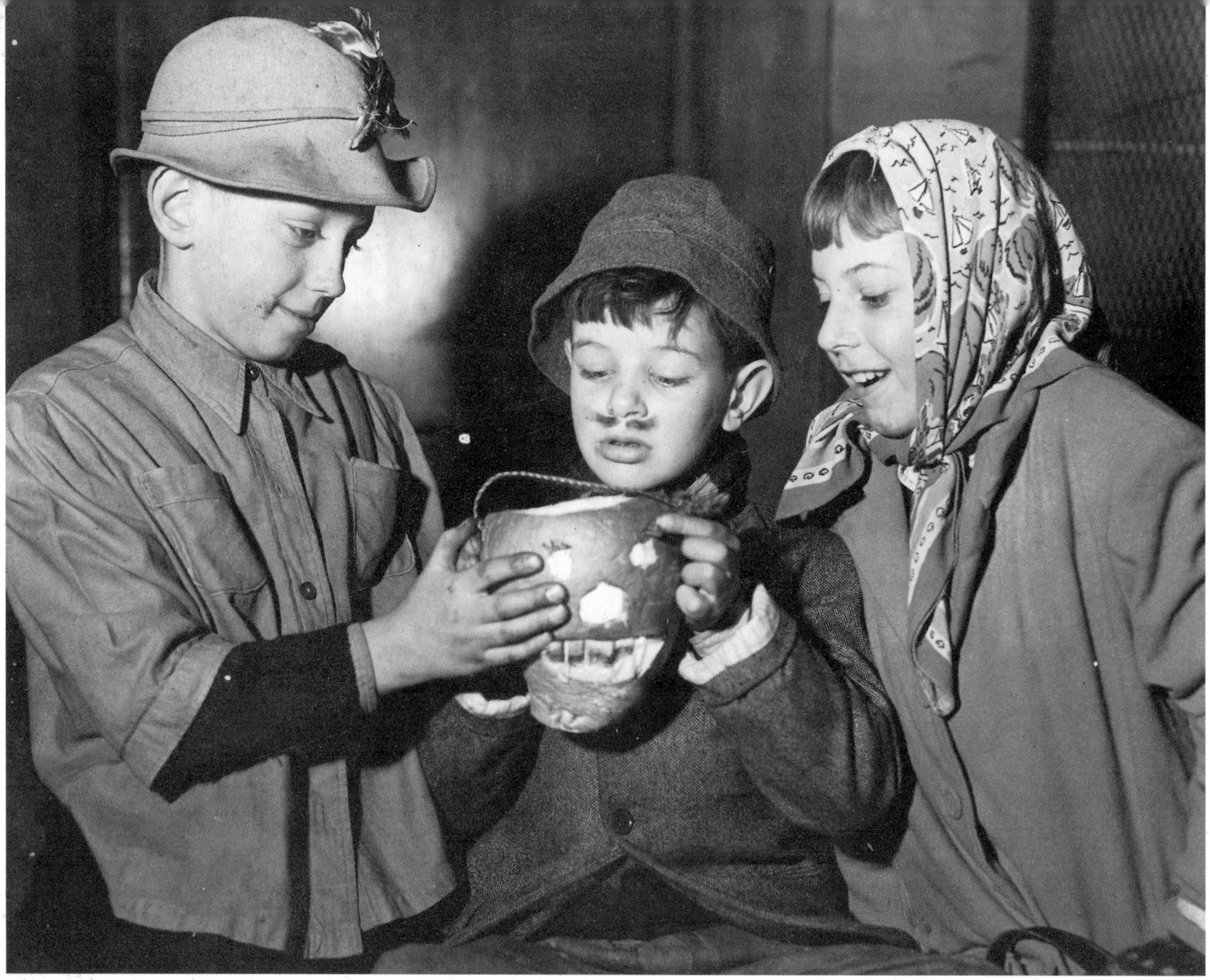

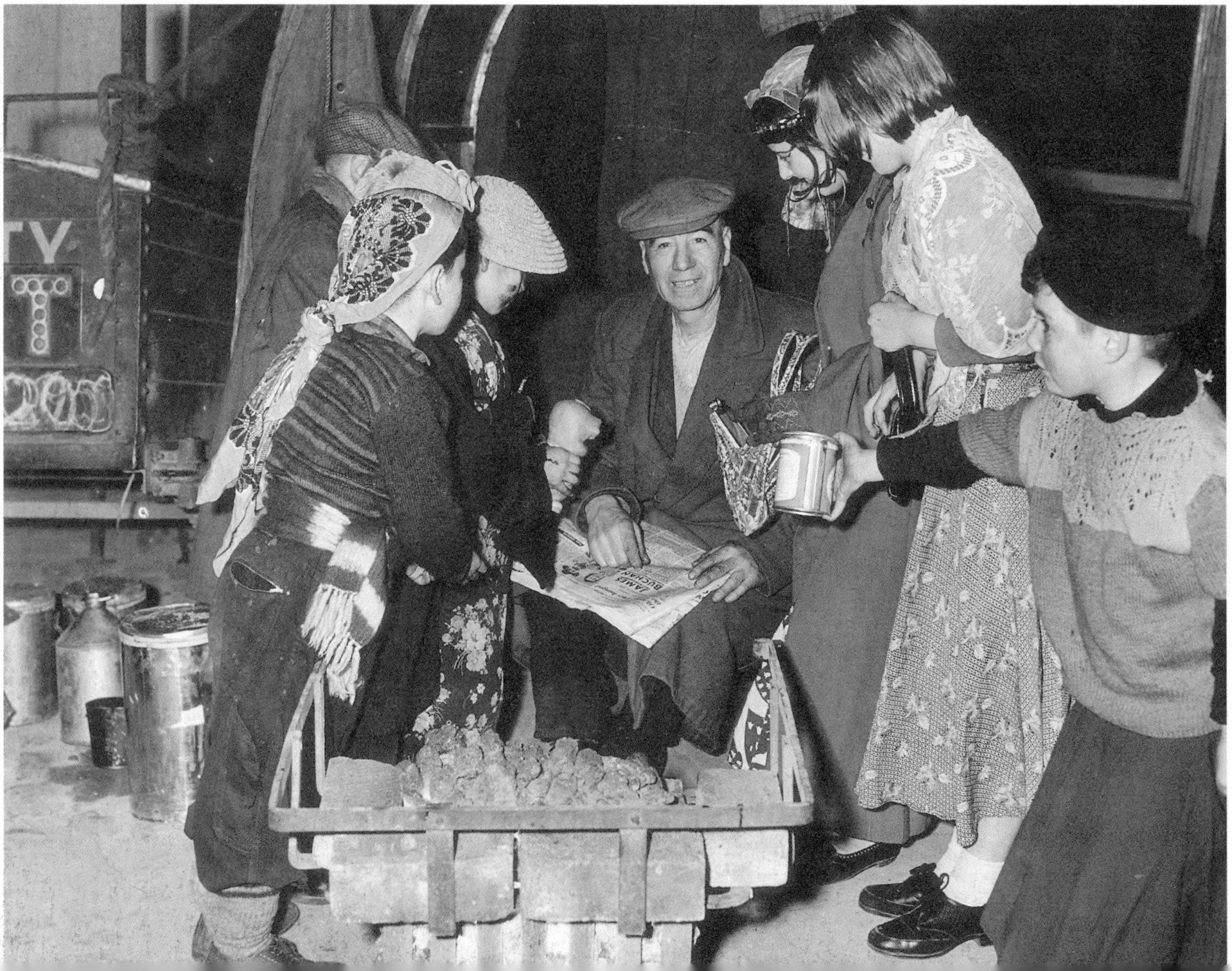

122. *opposite top:* Guisers with tumshie lanterns, Halloween 1956.

123. *opposite bottom:* Guisers in the Grassmarket look for a contribution from the nightwatchman.

124. Guisers, Leith.

125. A Halloween party at the Tweedie Memorial Boys' Club in the West Port, 1956. This Club enabled boys from all sorts of backgrounds to use a whole range of sports and hobby activities which were laid on. Here, 10 year-old George Ewens dooks for apples.

126. School's out — Morningside in 1954.

127. Young Norman Briggs on his first day at school in 1954. Guess who wants to go home.

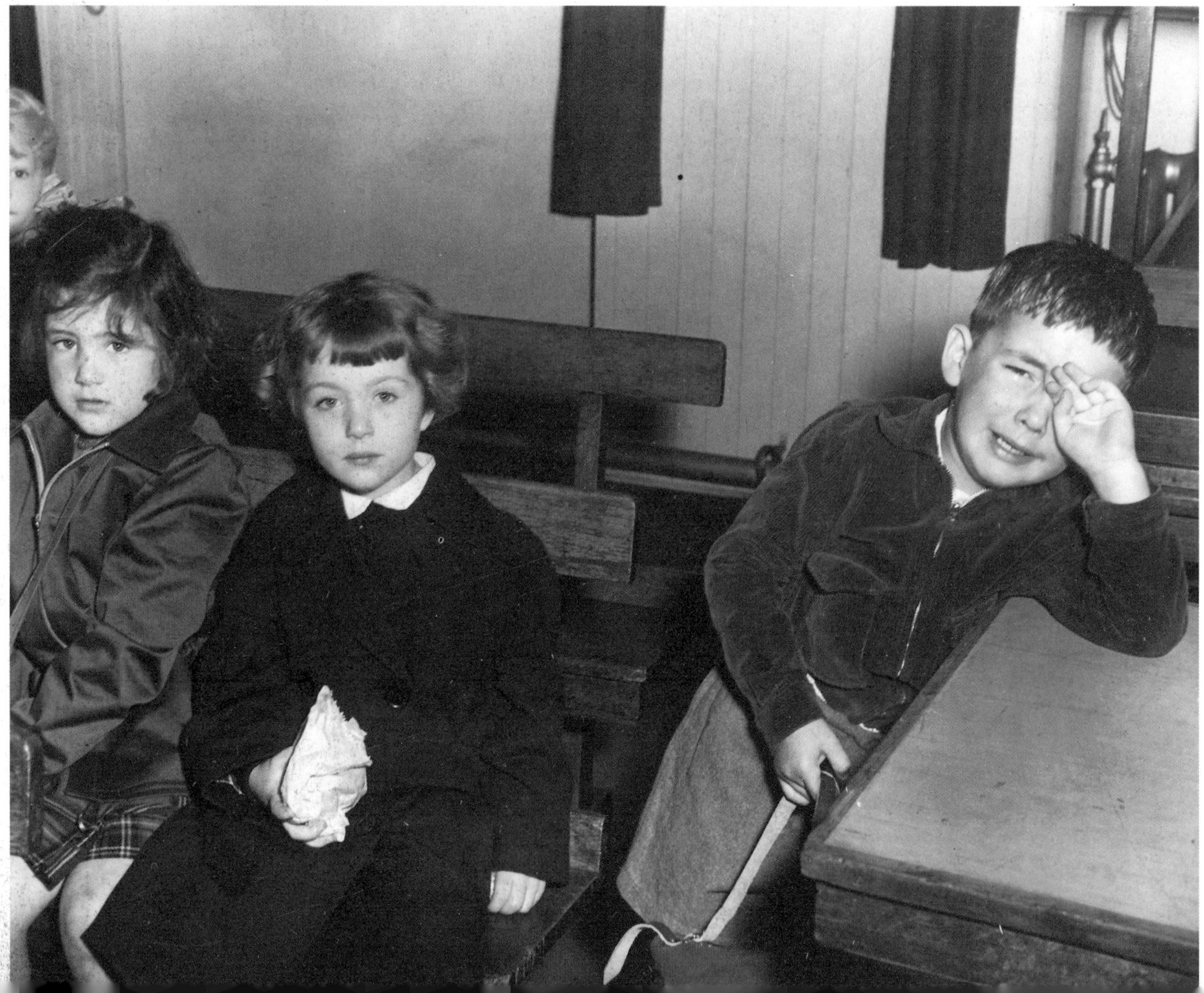

128. Lunchtime at Peffermill School (1954). Bangers and mash at your desk was the order of the day.

129. The Dining Room, Daniel Stewart's College (1958).

130. The closing concert of the year at St. Hilary's School in Morningside (July 1959).

131. Cookery class at Portobello Secondary (1953).

132. South Morningside School in the mid '50s: during this period the old tiered style of seating was replaced with a more modern layout.

133. Well known in the '50s as a regular cross-Forth swimmer, teacher Ned Barnie with his class at David Kilpatrick's School (1954).

134. An extraordinary photograph: class of twins at St. Cuthbert's School, February 1952. Schoolmaster Mr H Bocker is pictured with no less than 10 sets of twins who were at St Cuthbert's at that time. Surely, some sort of record . . . .

135. A view in the great hall at the opening of Duddingston Primary School (architects David Carr and Stuart Matthew), October 1958. Built to the latest design at the time, it boasted accommodation for 680 pupils, a full-sized football pitch and netball court. The *Evening News* reported, "Corridors, staircases and the exterior contain broad masses of bright colour."

AT WORK

The pattern of work in Edinburgh has changed radically since the 1950s. Much of the manufacturing base which still thrived then has now disappeared as exemplified by shipbuilding in Leith (146). Similarly, Leith has declined as a port as other methods of distribution like road transport became faster and more efficient (147—8).

Many of the more marginal workshop activities have also declined, like the making of fishing rods (151), wine bottling (143—5), and wigmaking (138). These economic pressures have also seen the decline and ultimate extinction of the Newhaven fishwife (140) and fishing from Newhaven (139). Changed tastes and fashions have seen off some other activities now rather peculiar to us today — like the painting of Humpty Dumpties on hot water bottles at the once great North British Rubber Co. (137) and the making of corsets (141) for a generation of women constricted into narrow waists and flat stomachs and behinds.

Unemployment was not, of course, the spectre that it is today, and the two youngsters pictured opposite could quite reasonably expect a lifetime of full employment — probably in the same job as they started their career in and almost certainly without moving away from their home city.

Patterns of wholesale buying and selling were also different in the days before electronic selling and futures markets in things as diverse as pork bellies and oranges. Men, and a few women, got together in open or covered markets and bid for each other's products, much as they had done for centuries, at the Corn Market in Gorgie (152) or the Fruitmarket in Market Street (153), the latter now the centre of the City's art community in the refurbished old premises.

For some, these changed patterns have brought extinction. Despite the European Community's purported effect of the breaking down of barriers, when did you last see a Breton onion man (154) cycling up Leith Walk or, for that matter, knocking on your door? Such a visit today would probably produce a request for an identity card, failing which a call to the local police station! Not only a sad reflection on the times we now live in, but an indication of how work activities have become 'streamlined' and shut out many small operators.

136. Their first jobs: milkboy John Barnyard and paper girl Margaret Cook on their rounds, October 1959.

137. Mrs Barker paints Humpty Dumpties on hot water bottles at the North British Rubber Co. (1958).

138. Wigmaking at the Adolph Theurer factory in Canonmills (1957).

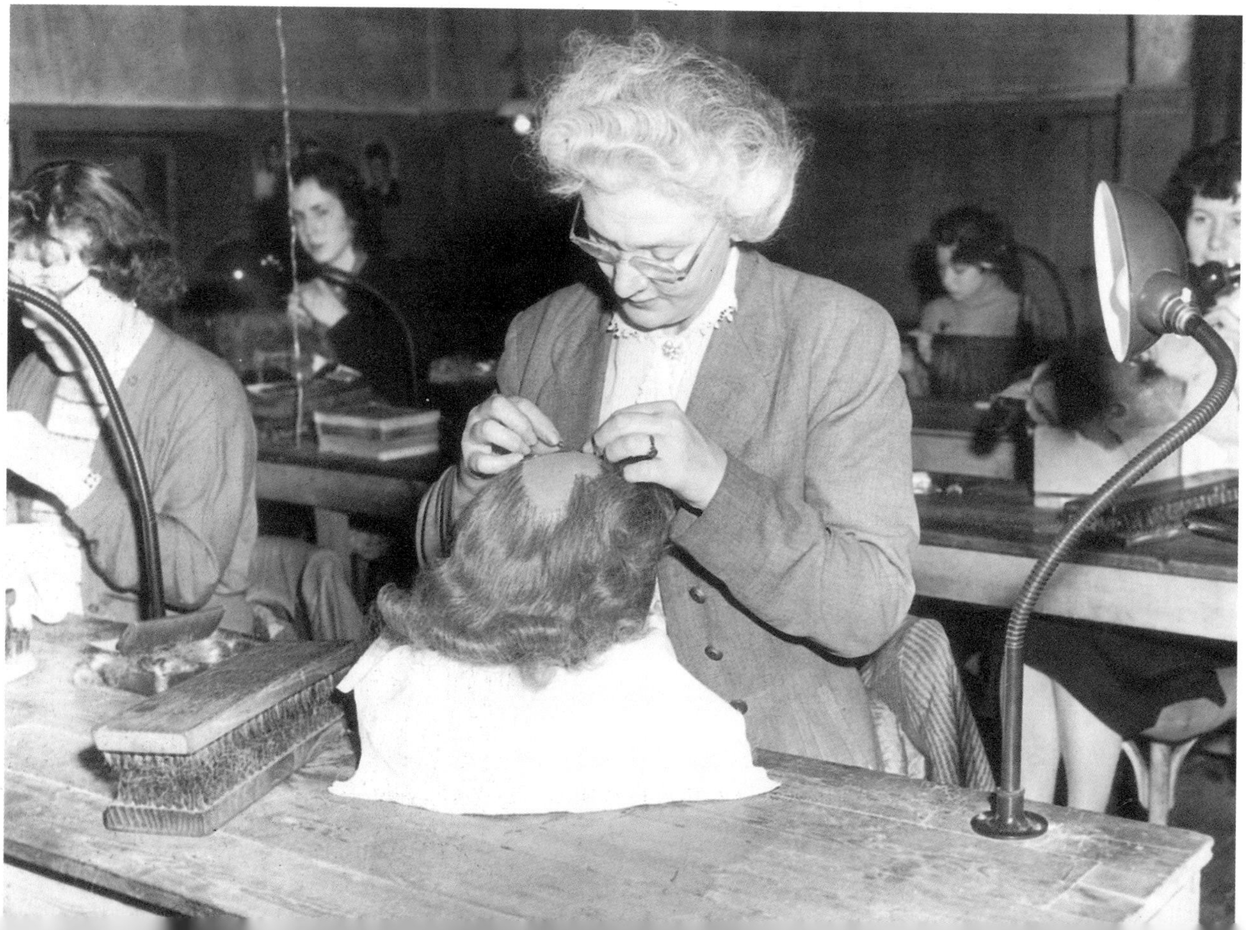

139. Fishing from Newhaven.

140. The last Newhaven fishwife, Mrs Esther Liston, pictured in 1962.

141. Sewers at work in Blair's corsetmaking department, Earl Grey Street (1962).

142. Stiff-upper-lip film star Jack Hawkins visits W & M Duncan's famous chocolate factory in Beaverhall Road.

143. In The Vaults at Leith in their 250th anniversary year in 1959: J G Thomson & Co still operated from The Vaults at that time, converted in the 1980s to flats, restaurant and a modern wine merchant's premises.

145. In Thomson's cellars.

4. Bottling wine in what was, in 1955, the West End's oldest wine merchants, Whigham, Ferguson & Cunningham, in Charlotte Square. The premises now house the Yuppie wine bar, Whighams, lunchtime haunt of Edinburgh's financial community.

146. Launch of the steamship *Cicero* at Leith, March 1954.
bottom right: Launch of the cargo steamer *Kaitoa* from Henry Robb's yard in February 1956. She was the seventh ship of this design built for the Union Steamship Co. of New Zealand.

147. Ten Centurion tanks for the Swedish armed forces are loaded at Leith Docks in April 1956. They arrived there from the Royal Ordnance Depot at Dalmuir and were loaded in what was regarded as the record time of two and a half hours.

148. Chairman of the Leith branch of the TGWU, Mr Henry Clark, addresses striking dockers, June 1956. Like most strikes of this time, it was a localised dispute arising out of an isolated grievance: in this case, the rate of pay for discharge of a cargo of sulphur. Nine hundred men were out and 12 ships were idle and the strike badly hit local grocers who, at that time, relied upon many fresh foodstuffs like bacon, eggs and butter being imported from Denmark via Leith.

149. The new headquarters for the National Union of Seamen, Maritime House, is opened on The Shore, August 1958. It also accommodated the National Assistance Board and the Ministry of Pensions which explains why it became known locally as 'the Golden Steps'. In 1984 the building was redeveloped into flats.

150. A waitress at the Chocolate House in the latest thing in uniforms: silver grey terylene dress with primrose bib and tucker. Note the up to the minute decor.

151. Making fishing tackle at Martins of Frederick Street (1957).

152. The Corn Exchange, Gorgie, in 1957.
It was an important trading market
for barley, wheat and oats in days of
less sophisticated communications.
It eventually closed in the mid-70s.

153. The old Fruitmarket in Market
Street caused many a traffic jam
(1954).

155. Cancelling banknotes by drilling through them at the British Linen Bank in Edinburgh.

154. *top left:* Onion men in Leith Walk (1955).

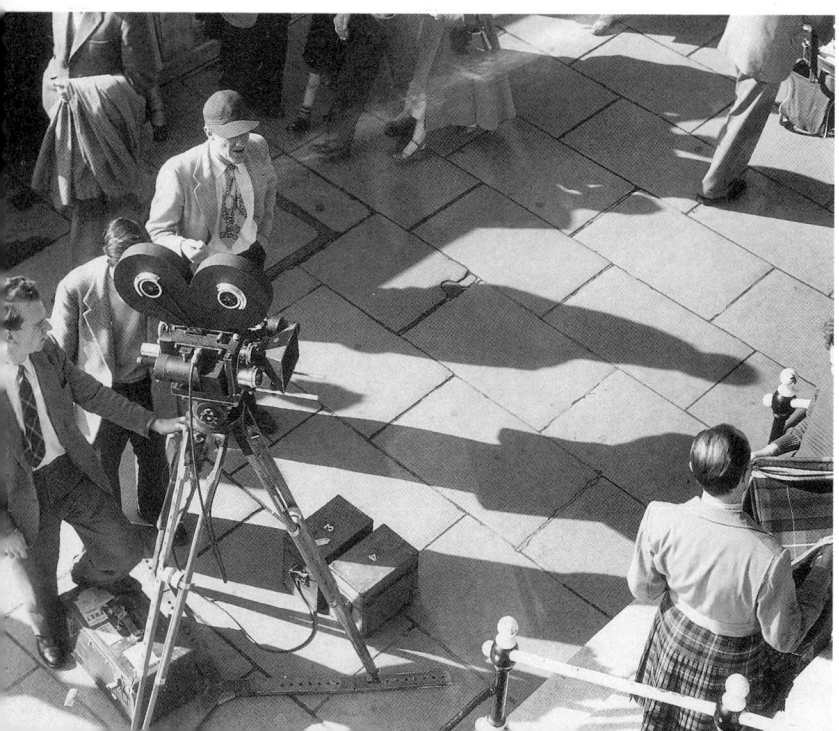

156. *top right:* Old style chimney sweeps John Martin and Davie Dykes worked the Leith, Granton and Restalrig areas of the City. John was the 'topper' — he did the roof work — and Davie the 'bottomer' who looked after the falling soot and the 'hee-heeing' up the lums. In 1961 the going rate was 7s 6d a chimney (37.5 new pence) and they reckoned to sweep 25 chimneys a day. *Dispatch* columnist John Gibson (*who he?)* described it then as an "ailing trade — youngsters simply can't be coaxed into the coal black role."

157. Sir Compton Mackenzie under the TV cameras (1957). 'Monty' used to live in Drummond Place and although he was an extremely prolific and erudite writer he was probably best known for his world famous comic novel *Whisky Galore*.

158. *Left:* A Pathe film crew shoot *The Festival City* in Edinburgh. September 1954.

THERE'S NO BUSINESS LIKE . . .

Television had yet to usurp the appeal of the live show and theatres including the Empire and the Palladium regularly offered the chance for Edinburgh people to see their idols. In the mid to late 50s British stars appeared to take over from their American counterparts who had held the centre stage. Singers like Johnny Rae (167) and Italo-Americans like Mario Lanza (169) were replaced in popular affection by the likes of Cliff Richard (160—61). Tommy Steele (162), Lonnie Donegan (165) and Adam Faith (163). British proponents of popular jazz were coming into their own: names like Humphrey Lyttelton (170), the Ted Heath Band (171), Eric Delaney (173) and Eddie Calvert (172), the Man with the Golden Trumpet who enjoyed a string of hits.

Both the Edinburgh Festival and the Edinburgh Film Festival started in 1947 and ever since have run concurrently, both bringing to the city a wide range of stars and personalities well known through stage and screen appearances. Personalities from the world of cinema like Orson Welles (190), Greer Garson (189), Gene Kelly (191), Cary Grant (197), Peter Sellers (196) and Bob Hope (195), were supplemented by emergent TV personalities like Jack Warner (175), Bernard Bresslaw (182), Lady Isobel Barnett (185) and Michaela Dennis (184).

Radio was a well-established medium — unassailable at on time in terms of popularity — and well respected personalities included Wilfred Pickles (188) and Ted Ray (181).

It is particularly fascinating to see some well-nigh legendary names in the Edinburgh of the 50s: Walt Disney (194), Victor Sylvester (186) and Laurel & Hardy (180) are all synonymous with the period.

And although the hero he was to later play had already achieved cult status, Edinburgh's own Sean Connery is as yet a relatively unknown although thoroughly competent actor . . . (187).

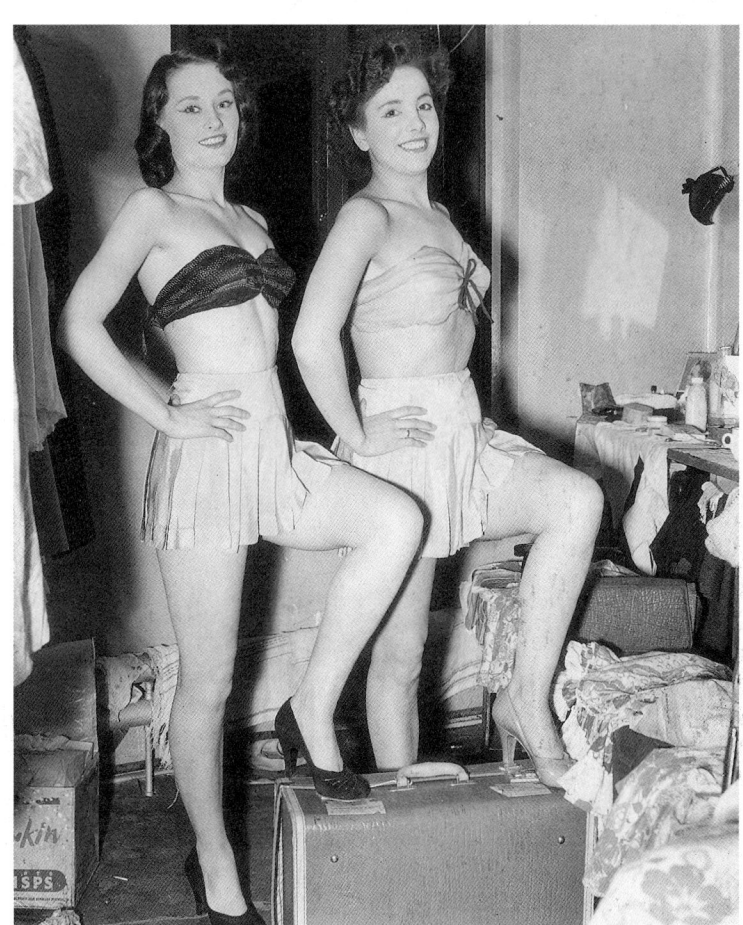

159.   Palladium girls (1954).

160. Cliff and two young fans, Denise Murphy and Kathleen McLaughlin, before his Edinburgh concert (1961).

161. Cliff Richard at the Usher Hall in 1961, at the peak of his popularity. His biggest hit in the 50s was *Got Myself a Crying, Walking, Sleeping, Talking Living Doll* (1959).

163. *bottom left:* Heart-throb department: Adam Faith (*Poor Me*) at Edinburgh Castle (1961).

162. Tommy Steele in Edinburgh in May 1958. According to his manager, he was recovering from a "mauling" by young fans after a concert in Dundee.

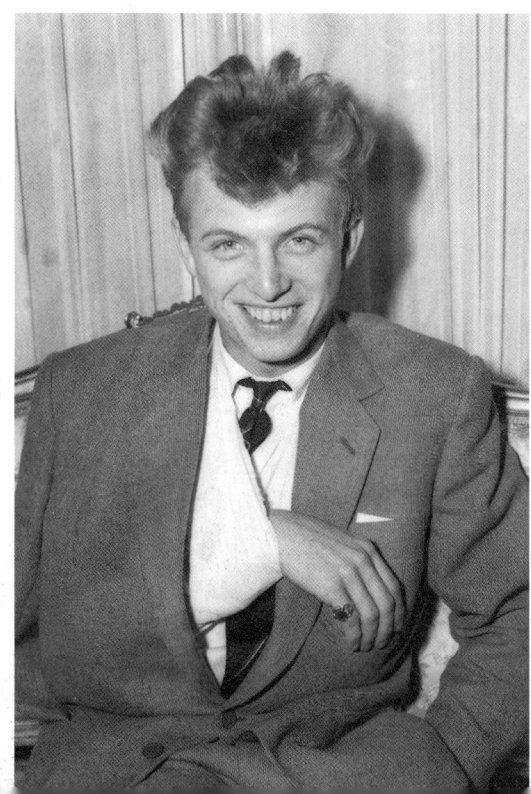

164. Folk singers Robin Hall and Jimmy MacGregor at The Howff (1961). This High Street hangout was much favoured by the folk fraternity. The duo were also appearing regularly at this time on the nightly news programme Tonight (1957—65), produced by Donald Baverstock and Alasdair Milne — the latter to become Director General at the BBC — and which was characterised by a new and easy going approach to current affairs.

165. Lonnie Donegan arrives for a rehearsal for his Edinburgh appearance (1958). Formerly Chris Barber's banjo player, his record *Rock Island Line* went to the top of the charts in 1956. It was the precursor of a string of hits including the immortal *Does your Chewing Gum lose its Flavour on the Bedpost Overnight?*, *Putting on the Style* and *Hang down your Head Tom Dooley*.

166. A new generation of pop stars was presaged by the arrival of The Beatles on the scene in 1963. Here they are photographed during their first visit to Edinburgh.

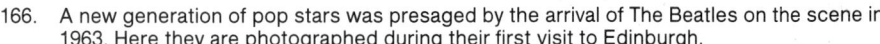

167. Laconically described as "a crooner who hails from America", Johnny Rae appeared at the Empire Theatre in May 1955. The *Dispatch* correspondent at the concert did admit later, however, that he had "an electric effect" on his largely female audience reducing it to screams and tears. Here he is pictured in his dressing room with one of his fans, Alice Murray. The Empire, in Nicolson Street, opened in 1928, was taken over by Mecca from Moss Empires in 1962 and although live shows were continued for a while the dreaded bingo was introduced. Previously, it had been a popular venue for live shows ranging from pop concerts to ballet.

168. *bottom left:* Wartime heart throb Vera Lynn in Edinburgh to meet Burma Veterans, September 1954.

169. American opera singer Singer Mario Lanza in characteristic pose at the Caledonian Hotel in March 1958. Hollywood's version of the great Italian tenor, he starred in *The Great Caruso* (1951) and *The Seven Hills of Rome* (1958). One year after this photograph was taken he was dead, having literally eaten himself to death.

0. Humphrehy Lyttelton appeared at the Usher Hall in 1957 at the height of the trad boom.

1. *top right:* The Ted Heath Band, the only British band to rival the preeminence of its American counterparts in the 50s, with Red Price the Rock 'n' Roll Tenor Sax Man, at the Usher Hall in September 1956.

2. *below:* Eddie Calvert — 'the Man with the Golden Trumpet' — had everyone whistling *Zambezi* at the Empire in March 1956.

3. *right:* English bandleader Eric Delaney at the Palais de Danse (1955). First and foremost a showman Delaney was renowned as a speciality drummer.

4. *bottom right:* Canadian born pianist Oscar Peterson pictured in Edinburgh in 1955 on one of his first visits to Britain. He was just becoming internationally known at this time.

175. Jack Warner at the Princess Margaret Rose Hospital to present toys for the Gaumont/Odeon scheme. His most famous role was as the aimiable, old fashioned P C George Dixon in, first of all, the film *The Blue Lamp* (1950) and, later, despite his demise at the end of the film, the TV series *Dixon of Dock Green.*

176. Actor Duncan Macrae opens the old peoples' lunch club in Cables Wynd, Leith (1956).

177. Claire Bloom and Richard Burton inspect the Edinburgh Festival programme in August 1953. Individually, they both enjoyed distinguished careers during the 1950s which they crowned together in *Look Back in Anger* in 1959. On Burton's left is Fay Compton.

178. Actor Richard Hearne, at that time popular with kids in his role as Mr Pastry, visits Patrick Thomsons.

179. Actress Shirley Ann Field was in Edinburgh in October 1960 to promote her new film *Beat Girl* in which she played opposite beatnik-playing Adam Faith. It was regarded as outrageous stuff at the time and carried an X certificate — which can be understood given Miss Field's undoubted charms. Faith himself described it as "no epic" and the only at all memorable part of it was his hit song *Someone Else's Baby*.

181. Comedian Ted Ray *(Ray's A Laugh)* and his family in Edinburgh.

180. Laurel and Hardy appeared at the Empire Theatre in April 1954. Here they tackle the current craze — the yo yo.

182. Actor Bernard Bresslaw visiting Dr Barnardo's Home in Balerno in 1959. He had just shot to stardom in Granada TV's comedy series *The Army Game*, in which he played an unfathomably stupid and goofy private soldier with the catchline, "I only arsked . . .". This line gave the title to a film in 1958. Records, TV spectaculars and more films followed.

183. Actor James Robertson Justice and actress Susan Beaumont photographed with Charities Queen Ann Morrison. They were in Edinburgh in 1958 for the screening of *Innocent Sinners*, a little item which has since passed into the mists of time.

184. TV safari personality Michaela Dennis signs copies of her book, *Leopard in My Lap*, at Elliotts Bookshop (1955). Together with her other half, Armand Denis, she was the first TV wildlife programme presenter and the heavy two-handed style of their programmes gave birth to much amusement and mimicry.

185. Lady Isobel Barnett, *of What's My Line?* fame, with fishermen at Newhaven in 1955. She was an enormously popular TV personality in the 50s: a writer in the *Radio Times* once described her as "the sort of person women liked to think their daughter would grow up into after she had married a titled millionaire". Which says much about the aspirations of the 50s. She tragically took her own life in 1981 after a shoplifting charge.

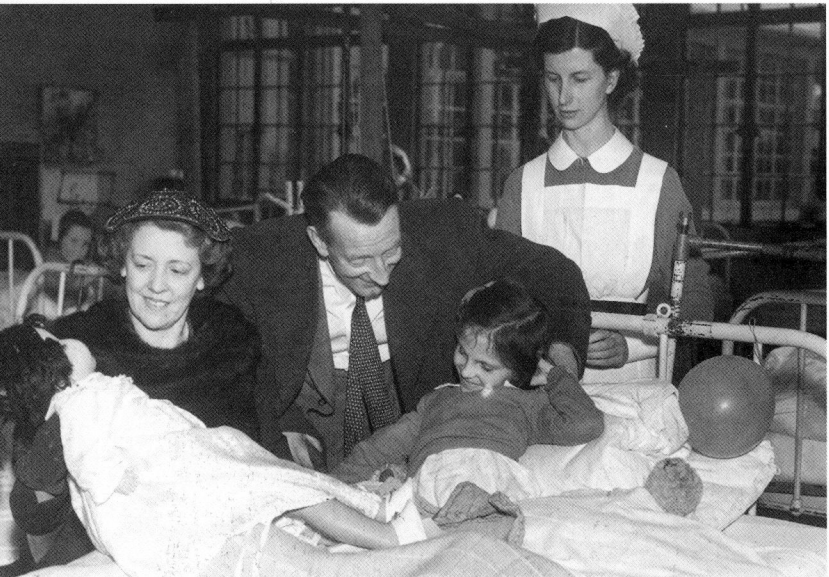

187. Actor Sean Connery in pre-Bond days (1959) at the Kings Theatre where he was appearing in *The Seashell*

186. *top left:* In April 1959 the maestro himself, Victor Sylvester, visited his dance studio in Edinburgh, danced with his pupils and signed copies of his new book *Dancing is My Life*.

189. Red-haired Anglo-Irish actress Greer Garson in Edinburgh in 1954. Appropriately enough, her latest film was appearing — *Strange Lady in Town*.

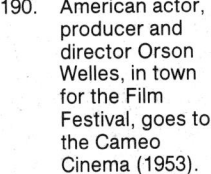

188. Wilfred Pickles and his wife Mabel, stars of radio's *Have A Go*, in Edinburgh. Millions waited for his Yorkshire-accented catchphrase every week, "Mabel, what's on the table?"

190. American actor, producer and director Orson Welles, in town for the Film Festival, goes to the Cameo Cinema (1953).

191. Gene Kelly and his producer Arthur Freed (who also wrote the lyrics of the unforgettable title number to the film *Singin in the Rain*) book into the Caledonian Hotel. Their long partnership gave a whole new meaning to the phrase 'splash hit'.

192. Comedian Terry-Thomas, film producer-director John Boulting and his wife photographed at the White Cockade Club in 1957. Comic actor Thomas worked with Boulting on a string of films in the 50s including army farce *Private's Progress* (1956) and the seminal *I'm All Right Jack* (1959) which expertly satirised so many aspects of British life in the 50s, setting the scene for the satire boom of the early 60s.

193. *top left:* Jackie Collins appearing on Carroll Levis TV *Star Search Show* at the Empire Theatre (1959).

194. *top right:* In July 1949 Walt Disney came to Edinburgh while he was making *Treasure Island* at Denham Studios. He is pictured here during his visit to Robert Louis Stevenson's birthplace at 8, Howard Place.

195. *left:* Bob Hope at Poole's Cinema (1952).

196. *above*: Peter Sellers plays the angry young man on arrival at Turnhouse, March 1960. He had come to Edinburgh to attend the premiere of *The Battle of the Sexes*, which was shot in Edinburgh.

197. Cary Grant in Edinburgh, 1958.

198. In August 1955 Dirk Bogarde visited Film House (then in Randolph Crescent) to attend a showing of *Doctor at Sea*, the second of a highly successful series of Doctor films in the 50s.

199. Veronica Hurst at a showing of the 1954 film *Angels One Five* together with Group Captain J A Brown.

200. Filming the Betty Box production of *The Thirty Nine Steps* on the Forth Railway Bridge, on a quiet Sunday in September 1958. Kenneth More starred in this, the second production of the John Buchan yarn. Although a successful effort it did not match the 1934 version starring Robert Donat and Madeleine Carroll. In the 1958 version Richard Hannay was hunted for nuclear secrets after some rewriting.

201. American comedian Red Skelton at Turnhouse Airport with his family, August 2 1957. He was making a round the world trip to seek medical treatment for his son Richard (left) who was dying of luekaemia.

TRANSPORT EXPLOSION

202.　This was deemed "severe traffic congestion" in Princes Street in 1953!

Public transport was the way to work and the shops in 1950 although, as the decade wore on, the private motor car became an increasingly important conveyance and symbol of improved affluence. What were perceived as traffic and parking problems at that time now seem laughable to us (202—3) and the transport policies of the time were patently misled in the light of history.

The tram was scrapped in Edinburgh starting with the Gorgie depot, the last tram in the city running in 1956 (205—11). Although not without criticism at the time for many travellers reckoned the motor bus increased journey times across the city and only served to worsen congestion; and now there was just the choice of motor bus (213—16) or rail. There was still a network of rail stations serving the citizens of Edinburgh although extensive closures came into force in 1962, even before the visit of Dr Richard Beeching (234).

Some alarming new street furniture made its appearance (229—30) and, alas, the parking meter was here to stay. The dramatic rise in the numbers and types of vehicles on the road had set the seal, once and for all, on unrestricted parking. Local traders forecast ruin, British Rail offered parking to commuters at Princes Street Station, and, initially, motorists boycotted the meter areas in George Street, Charlotte and St Andrew Squares. But the much disliked innovation became accepted within a short time.

In 1950, curiously, the flying boat was seen as the way ahead for air transport. *The Scotsman* reported in July 1949 that 'British flying boats look like putting us in front of the world again'. This euphoric prediction was not borne out by the Leith-London service which started the following year and lasted but a few months (239). Instead, Turnhouse became the hub for the capital's air connections with London and a new terminal was opened (243) and in 1961 there were further extensive improvements to facilitate the use of the 100-passenger Vanguard, the so-called 'colossus of the air' at the time.

203. *top left:* Traffic congestion in George Street. Motorists were already complaining of parking difficulties in the early 50s.

204. *top right:* Points control box for trams (1951).

205. *left:* Specially decorated for the occasion, Edinburgh's last tramcar passes the King's Theatre, November 13 1956.

206. As late as 1961, tram rails were still being removed — in this instance, in Salisbury Place. On the drill is Hugh Burns who is working in a 'muffle box' so as not to disturb nearby patients at Longmore Hospital.

07. Tram rails are removed in Slateford Road, July 1953.

08. *top right:* Inside the last no. 28 tram, November 1956.

09. Just a week after the last tram has passed, the tram rails are removed in Princes Street in November 1956.

10. *bottom:* Tram rails are removed in London Road, June 1955.

11. *bottom right:* The last Corstorphine tramcar, July 1954

![Burning trams](top image)

212.   A sad end as Edinburgh trams are destroyed at Coatbridge (October 1956).

213.   No. 26 bus on fire in Princes Street, August 1957. The sight of this no doubt gave succour to all the supporters of the recently deposed tram!

214.   An object of curiosity upon introduction in 1954 — the bell push

215. Scottish Omnibuses opened their brand new station in Clyde Street in April 1957. It incorporated subways which were regarded as a revolutionary experiment in pedestrian safety.

216. Five of these new 72-seater 'superbuses' were bought by Edinburgh Corporation Transport at the beginning of 1959.

217. The bubble car must be one of the most enduring images of the 50s. There was a bubble car parade during Edinburgh University Students' Charities Week in 1959 and it featured these models seen stepping out of an Isetta bubble car fresh from the student fashion show — a regular event at that time during Charities Week.

218. This brand new, smoke grey Dodge Phoenix was known as the "Sputnik" car, pictured here outside Gilroy's Garage. It came to Edinburgh for the *Evening Dispatch* 'Concours d'Elegance' in 1960. It was desribed as "the slickest, biggest, mostest car" and was regarded as remarkable because it had an early automatic gearbox — "It almost drives itself. It is impossible not to have one's ego boosted in this car", swooned the *Dispatch's* motoring correspondent.

219. A 1935 Rolls Royce was 'cannibalised' by Mr T Spence of the Grove Garage to form this breakdown truck in 1960.

The new showrooms of Fiat dealers Spey Motors in Leith Walk, 1959.

221. The new Morris Oxford is admired by motor agents at Westfield, May 1954.

222.   *top left:* Self-drive hire — in style. SMT Garage in Haymarket, 1956.

223.   A shipment of 40 Czechoslovakian Skodas arrive at Leith's Imperial Dock, 1960.

225.   *top right:* The Ford Anglia, a classic small family car of the 50s with 3-speed gearbox, side-valve engine and vacuum wipers — which tended to stop when you went uphill.

224.   Cochranes' Garage, South Trinity Road, 1960.

226. Alexanders held a five day motor show in Waverely Market in June 1956 at which they exhibited 100 Ford motor cars and commercial vehicles worth, at the time, an incredible £ 100,000. Attention was focussed on the new Zephyr, Zodiac and Consul models although smaller cars like the Anglia, Prefect and Squire were still the most popular with motorists.

227. The introduction of the Mini Minor in 1959 was something of a sensation. Issigoni's design was revolutionary for its time and the car quickly assumed widespread popularity as motorists reacted to the petrol guzzling large American type of cars which had been so popular in the late 50s. This car was on display in Princes Street in August 1959. The model was Marion Wyllie Davies.

228. *previous* Laying the electric blanket at the foot of the Mound in 1959. A surface coating of tar and grit is being laid over a network of electrical wiring. The operation made a big difference in negotiating the steep climb in ice and snow!

"What aboot a walk up the Mound tae get oor feet warm?"

229. Parking meters are erected in George Street, July 1962.

230. In October 1960 this was the first parking meter ever to be seen in Edinburgh. It was erected for display purposes outside the City Chambers in the High Street. It aroused much curiosity at the time but no one could tell then what a major feature of motorists' life it was to become.

231. In the late 50s the increased number of vehicles on the road necessitated major road improvements. Here the Wallyford roundabout is under construction, which entailed the reconstruction of the main line railway tunnel.

232. Crowds at Waverley Station during the July 1957 bus strike — in the days when there was still a viable rail option for commuters living in Edinburgh suburbs.

233. Queue for buses in St Andrew Square. April 1954.

234. Probably one of the most denigrated figures in the whole history of British transport, Dr Beeching, leaves Waverley Station in August 1962 on his study trip out of which grew his recommendations to axe much of the rail network.

235. Caledonian engine no. 123 in the Caledonian Station on Princes Street before a special trip to Carlisle in August 1958 to commemorate the Edinburgh-London railway race of 1888.

236. The last diesel train to run on the north Leith suburban line leaves Princes Street, April 30 1962. The Edinburgh suburban circle line and rail services to Bonnyrigg and Rosewell closed later in the year. Stations then open at Morningside Road, Duddingston, Newington, Blackford Hill, Craiglockhart and Gorgie East all closed on September 10. Mr Ernest Marples, the Minister of Transport, said that the closures would save £ 57,000 a year.

237. The first diesel train on the Edinburgh—Glasgow route arrives from British Railways Swindon workshops in August 1956, the beginning of the end for the steam engine. As an engine driver wrote at the time, "you don't need to hang out the side window any longer listening to 'the beat', you sit in armchair comfort and look at a few dials."

238. The Talisman express train passes through Portobello Station on its first run to Kings Cross in September 1956.

239. An Aquila Air Services Sunderland flying boat in Leith Harbour after the maiden flight of the short-lived London-Leith flying boat service, June 1950. At the time this was seriously reckoned to be the future of air passenger transport . . .

240. Jill Morgan, a BEA air hostess of the mid 50s at Turnhouse Airport.

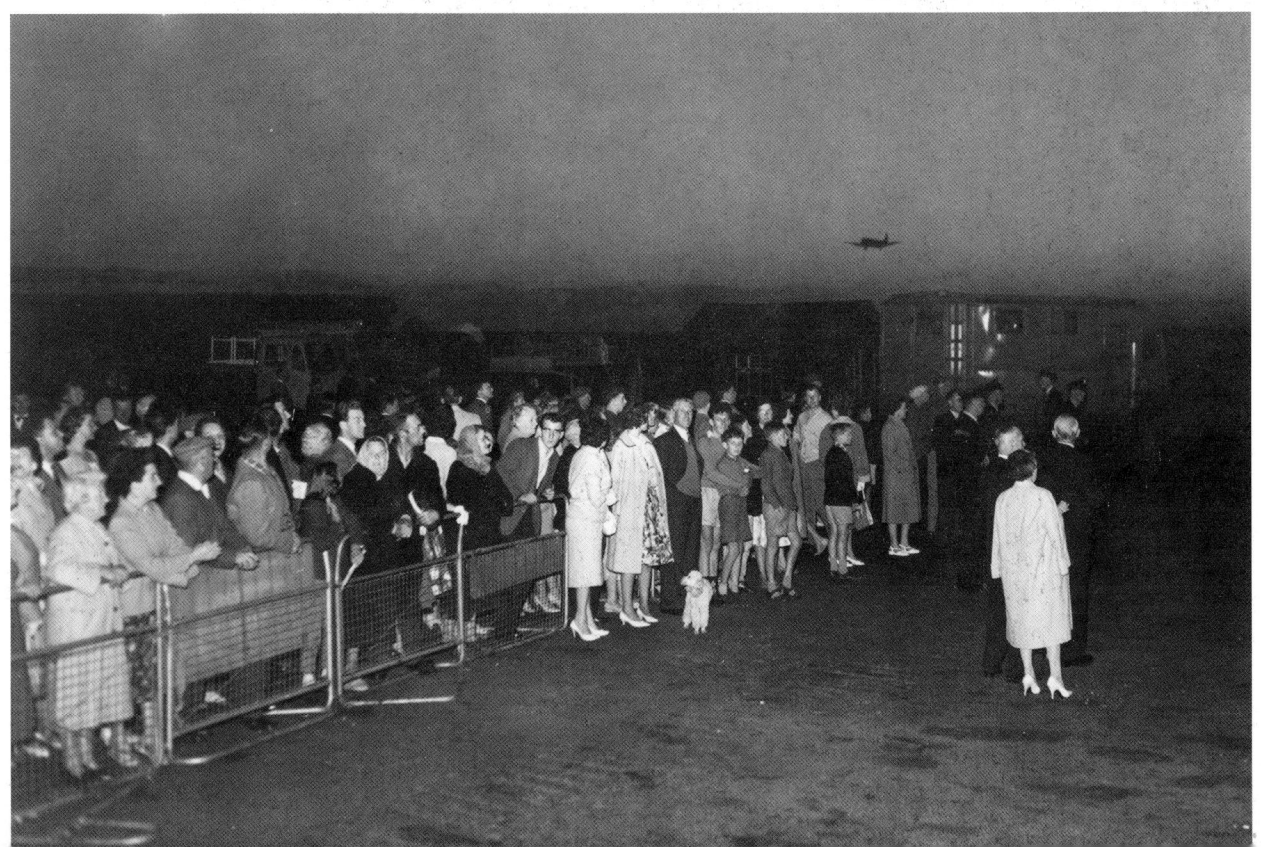

241. The derelict airfield at East Fortune was brought into use as a temporary airport for Edinburgh in April 1961 whilst improvements were made to the runway at Turnhouse so that it could handle the BEA Vanguards. Here air traffic controllers make their final preparations in the renovated East Fortune control tower.

242. As the temporary airport is closed down at the end of July 1961, the last BEA Viscount takes off. During the four months of operation, the airfield handled 2,640 aircraft movements and 96,000 passengers were carried. East Fortune now houses the Royal Scottish Museum's 'Museum of Flight', and a popular weekend market.

243. The new £ 75,000 terminal at Turnhouse Airport, April 1956. The new building was described as "ultra modern" in design and furnishings. The buildings it replaced had been built in 1934 as barrack blocks for service personnel.

244. Harbinger of the future: the Forth Road Bridge under construction. The twin towers rise on both sides of the Forth, November 1960.

HOLD THE FRONT PAGE!

245. Caught in the wind at Waverley Steps . . . A favourite subject for picture editors on North Bridge through the decades.

The interests of newspaper readers have not changed dramatically over the decades, although there has been much change in the manner of presentation of the news. Dynamic Canadian newspaper proprietor Roy Thomson bought *The Scotsman* and *The Evening Dispatch* out of private control in 1953 and shook the papers up out of all recognition. In 1957, the classified ads disappeared off the front page (276) of the former paper — a revolution in itself — and the latter abandoned its tabloid size in October 1959. It never caught up with the *Evening News*, however, and in 1963 Thomson felt obliged to acquire the *News* — and close the *Dispatch*.

In the days when newspapers only printed the news that was fit to print, there was much respectful reporting of royalty (246—50). The nearest to sensation seeking in the 50s must have been the reporting of the Patino elopement (251—2) which was the subject of enormous press interest and the eloping couple — poor little rich children — were pursued around Scotland by irate father, private detectives and the denizens of the press.

The usual patchwork of fires (264—5), crashes (265—8) and personalities like Billy Graham (259) and the indefatigable Barbara Moore (257) filled the papers although there were some phenomena unknown today. The smash and grab raid is as extinct as a crime (260) as hanging is as a penalty (262—3), and the sight of derailed steam locomotives is a memory for which only the most perverse of nostalgics will yearn (271—74).

246. *top left:* While Edinburgh slept one early Sunday morning in May 1953 there was this rehearsal for the Coronation visit.

247. The salute to mark the Coronation of Queen Elizabeth II is fired from Edinburgh Castle, June 1953.

248. Her Majesty the Queen visits the Royal College of Nursing in Heriot Row, 1952.

249. *bottom left:* The state carriage with Her Majesty and Prince Philip during the Coronation visit of Queen Elizabeth II to Edinburgh.

250. Her Majesty the Queen leaves Register House during the 1952 Royal visit to Edinburgh.

251. Reporters and photographers congregated outside Prestonfield House in January 1954 to cover the Patino elopement story. For weeks it was headline news all over the country after James Goldsmith and Miss Maria Isabel Patino eoloped to Scotland. Her father, a Bolivian tin mining millionaire, pursued them to Scotland and tried to prevent the marriage of his 18 year-old daughter to the 20 year-old son of a director of the Savoy Hotel. In Edinburgh they stayed at Prestonfield House, then still a private home, with Mr and Mrs Roderick Oliver.

252. Mr and Mrs James Goldsmith after their Edinburgh marriage on January 8. After having been pursued across Scotland by private detectives and legal action in the Court of Session to prevent the marriage, they became celebrities, pursued relentlessly throughout Edinburgh by the world's press.

254. Wendy Wood and the Scottish Patriots objected to the assisted emigration scheme offered by the Australian government whereby, at the end of the 50s, Scots were emigrating at the rate of over 40,000 a year for only £ 10 passage money. They burned application forms and danced an eightsome reel outside the newly set up Australia office in St Andrew Square (1959).

253. *top left:* In 1956 Dr Neumann, inventor of polyfilla, came to Edinburgh and demonstrated what, at that time, was a well nigh unbelievable invention.

255. American Abbot du Gally visited Edinburgh in August 1955 on his round the world bicycle ride. It was, in reality, a somewhat leisurely peregrination: he had started in 1951 and aimed to complete it in 1960. Nobody seems to know whether or not he was successful. Maybe he's still at it . . .

256. Colonel Sir John Hunt, leader of the Everest expedition, receives the Livingstone Medal in the Usher Hall (1953).

Dr Barbara Moore on Soutra Hill en route for London: the intrepid woman champion of the long distance marchers, the 56-year-old doctor walked to London without sleep. It was reported, with a great deal of surprise, that she lived on a diet of fruit, vegetable juices and honey — long before such a regime was accepted as being healthy. In the 50s she was regarded as a crank. "I am doing it for publicity," said Dr Moore referring darkly to her "superman secrets". After arriving in London she was admitted to hospital with blistered feet and suffering from exhaustion.

258. Endurance athletes of another sort, Ned Barnie and John Smith prepare to swim the Forth between Granton and Burntisland in July 1955. John Smith (19) was the youngest swimmer ever to achieve this and, indeed, only three other swimmers had ever managed the swim. Portobello teacher Ned Barnie was an old hand having accomplished the swim on five occasions — once there and back. Here the duo are greased down before setting off. The 7 mile swim took them four hours and twenty minutes. The *Dispatch* man reported that "Ned came in . . . looking as unconcerned as though he had done a length at Portobello Baths."

259. American evangelist Dr Billy Graham at Tynecastle Park for his open air meeting together with his wife and the Rev. Dr. Gunn. Billy Graham's splendidly orchestrated British tour in 1955 took the country by storm as thousands of Britons took the opportunity to come forward at his meetings for "a personal encounter with Christ". He used to declare, "I am selling the greatest product in the world." In fact, he used to be a Fuller Brush salesman and he promoted Christ as well as brushes or soap.

260. A common form of crime in the 1950s was the smash and grab raid. This was the aftermath of a raid on Holmwoods, jewellers in George Street (1958).

261. *below left:* An early armoured car service featured the assistance of a hound called Hector (1961).

262. *bottom left:* In October 1958 convicted murderer Donald Forbes married his girlfriend Margaret McLean in Saughton Prison. Here she leaves the prison in a car driven by the Rev. John Wood, the prison chaplain who married the pair amidst some controversy. This was the first time a condemned man had been married in a Scottish prison. A Glasgow millionaire gave the bride a cheque for the then amazing sum of £ 1000 as a wedding present.

263. The execution notice of Alexander Robertson, the Tron Square murderer, November 1954. He stabbed to death his divorced wife and 18 year-old son in their tenement home at 57 Tron Square. "Neighbours shuddered with horror at the gruesome evidence of the struggle, the bloodstained prints on the ground leading across one side of the square being those of bare feet," reported the *Evening News.*

264. A fire in Bristo Street above the old Parkers store (1960).

265. One of the most dramatic fires of the time was the blaze at C & A's Princes Street store in November 1955.

266. A motor car is lifted by crane from the Water of Leith at The Shore. This part of the Water was still navigable at the time, April 1958. Behind are the National Union of Seamens' headquarters building (now Maritime House) and the old Imperial Bar (now the Shore Bar and Restaurant).

267. The sad aftermath of a motor lorry accident outside the Kings Theatre (1959).

268. A blizzard was to blame for this van and car smash in Leith Walk, 1960.

269.   Victim of a sudden storm in July 1957, the pleasure boat *Skylark* off Portobello.

270.   The Forth ferry *Sir William Wallace* hard aground in February 1958. Fifty passengers were taken off by
        lifeboat after the fully laden morning ferry to Fife grounded on a rock: motorists had to abandon their cars
        and lorry drivers their loads whilst the vessel was refloated.

271. An engine is derailed at No. 19 Platform, Waverley Station, August 1957.

272. The Abbeyhill Railway Bridge collapsed just after completion on February 17 1958. The collapse happened at Brand Place just after it had been moved into position to replace the old wrought iron bridge. Train services between Leith and Waverley were disrupted.

273. Train accident at the mouth of Calton Tunnel in February 1955.

274. A runaway train smashed into the buffers at the old Caledonian Station, at the west end of Princes Street, and leapt thirty feet onto the platform in January 1958. "Steam hissed from the boiler and water poured from the safety valve." Although the first two carriages were derailed there were, fortunately, only minor injuries.

275. The first meeting of the new board of *The Scotsman* in March 1957. Roy Thomson at the head of the table with fellow directors Coltart, Whitton, Munro and Muir.

276. *top right:* Classified ads are off the front page of *The Scotsman* on April 17 1957. Canadian proprietor of the paper, Roy Thomson, looks at the first copy of the revamped paper. He had acquired a majority shareholding in The Scotsman Publications Ltd in 1953 and eventually became the sole owner. In November 1963 he added the *Evening News* to the stable which included *The Scotsman, The Weekly Scotsman* and *The Evening Dispatch*.

277. Telephonists at *The Scotsman* (1959).

278. Delivery vans at the despatch department.